"I love this book because it's so easy to read and filled with such common sense. It's bound to be the book of the decade to help people in all their relationships."
Patricia Fripp, CPAE, San Francisco, CA
Past President of National Speakers Assoc.

"Of all the relationship books I have read, this one stands out with its simple yet profoundly insightful concepts that cultivate value, trust, and joy in our relationships. I am devouring this book!"
David N. Wright, DMD, Fellow, International College of Dentists

"The powerful simplicity of this book is rare and compelling. Every parent, spouse, friend, employer, employee—everyone concerned with how they relate to any other human being—needs this message. The world would be a safer, friendlier, better place to live if we all practiced the validation process taught in this book. I am committed to it on a level that I know will change my life for the better."
Darla Hanks Isackson
Author, Editor, Mother of 5 sons

"When you come right down to it, everything that really matters is found in relationships. This book offers a powerful "user-friendly" repair tool— a straightforward and honest way to build and strengthen each other."
Thomas Myers, M.D.

"I want to turn the clock back thirty years and have another crack at raising my children using the principles I've learned in this book—relinquishing my role as 'Mrs. Fix-it' and allowing them to feel, grow, and problem-solve more independently. Still, I can use it now because it works like a charm with grown children, grandchildren, aged parents, and especially my spouse. Most importantly it relieves me of the responsibility to be all things to all people."
Janice Kapp Perry, Composer
Vice President, Prime Recordings

"It's given me something appropriate to say in difficult circumstances when I didn't know what to say when people poured their hearts out to me. I'm so grateful for this book. It's brought me great relief."
Maureen Bliss, Overton, NV

"It's amazing how much the concepts in your book have improved my business. My customers love me now!"
Mark C., Sales rep., San Diego, CA

"These validating principles have been enormously helpful in working with my patients, staff, and family members. Everyone needs to read this book."
Penny Fuehrer, R.N., Behavioral Medicine

"I see many financially successful people as clients in my Life Balance Coaching business. One of the most difficult challenges they face is personal relationships with those they care about. This book has assisted them in identifying their problems and has provided help in a clear, concise, and easy to follow manner. It is a great help that everyone needs."
Leo A. Weidner, Life Balance Coach
Author of *LifeCourse*

"In using validation when caring for my elderly parents, I notice a calming and peaceful feeling come over them. The argumentativeness and frustration dissolve and they seem to feel I understand. I used to think I had to make everything all better for them."
Garna Fitzgerald, Primary caregiver to elderly parents

"These concepts help us release ourselves from burdens we don't need to carry, allowing us to become our best selves. I have given this book to all of my married children."
Don C. Andrews, Colonel, U.S. Army, Retired

"Validation is great! It even works with my two-year-old. I can hardly believe how effective it is."
Diane Nel, Cosmetologist

"For my entire life I have been a 'pleaser.' Reading this book has given me the answers and ability to realize I do not have to please every one all the time, and, at the same time, I don't have to feel guilty. I can think of several people I'm going to give this book to. It's sure to be a national best seller!"
Cora Beutler, CEO, Publishers Distribution Center

"I'm underlining and reviewing—even memorizing—parts of this book. It's been significantly helpful to me."
Jeannine Peterson, Homemaker

"This is a great relationship training manual. It can improve the quality of life for all those who read it and apply the principles. It's jam packed with great truths between its covers."
Joyce H. Brown, Ph.D.
Author of *Heavenly Answers for Earthly Challenges*

I DON'T HAVE TO MAKE EVERYTHING ALL BETTER

I DON'T HAVE TO MAKE EVERYTHING ALL BETTER

Gary B. Lundberg
Marriage and Family Therapist

Joy Saunders Lundberg
Author, Poet, Lyricist

Riverpark Publishing Company
Las Vegas, Nevada

ISBN 0-915029-02-2
First Edition   1st Printing   September 1995
                   2nd Printing   January 1996
                   3rd Printing   August 1996
                   4th Printing   April 1997

Publisher: Riverpark Publishing
               4603 Imperial Beach Ave
               North Las Vegas, NV 89030
               1-800-224-1606

Cover design by Evan Twede

Publisher's Catalog in Publication

Lundberg, Gary B.
    I don't have to make everything all better / Gary B. Lundberg, Joy Saunders
Lundberg. -- 1st ed.
    p. cm.
    Includes bibliographical references.
    ISBN 0-915029-02-2

    1. Interpersonal relationships. 2. Self-actualization (Psychology) I.
Lundberg, Joy Saunders. II. Title.
HM132.L86 1996   158'.1
                                           QB196-40251

foreword

At times I grow weary of hearing psychology from some professionals who are clearer examples of abnormal psychology, spinning psychological concoctions to social problems as an alchemist concocts gold from lead—and with much the same results.

I Don't Have To Make Everything All Better is not that kind of a book. There is a pleasant absence of snake oil solutions to real problems. Rather, in the tradition of such classics as Dr. Scott Peck's *The Road Less Traveled* and Stephen R. Covey's *Spiritual Roots of Human Relationships*, the Lundbergs' book gives a direct, functional approach to improving relationships and bringing greater joy into our homes and lives.

It is always refreshing to be surprised by the obvious, and, more importantly, it is empowering to know that we can improve our circumstances.

If relationships came with an owner's manual, this is it.

Richard Paul Evans
New York Times Best-Selling Author of
The Christmas Box

Preface

For the past few years my wife, Joy, and I have been presenting seminars on the principles and concepts addressed in this book. Following these presentations many people have asked if we had a book with these ideas and have expressed disappointment when we did not. We have heard many say, "Please write it. I know it will help me and my family." Others have said, "I have a friend who desperately needs this. Please write the book." With that repeated encouragement and a desire to share what we have discovered, we have finally written it.

The basis of the concepts we cover come from a variety of sources. Each of our families of origin has given us a little different perspective and belief in mankind. Joy grew up on a farm in the western United States with seven brothers and one sister and I grew up in a large eastern city with two brothers. We had different lifestyles of moderate and humble surroundings. However, we were taught to believe that most people are good and trustworthy. The wide variety of neighbors and business associates we have met have continued to confirm these beliefs and have helped us instill them in our children.

As I studied for my masters degree, the professors introduced additional concepts and ideas. Some meshed with my personal beliefs. I found myself testing parts of the many different psychological theories to find those that fit my personality. I extended these ideas through study and application in my Marriage and Family Therapy practice and developed the six principles outlined in this book. Joy has tried and proved them as well and has become as much an advocate of them as I am. Applying these concepts has helped us as we have struggled with problems much like any other married couple.

We believe in the concepts presented in our book because of the positive changes they have made in our own life and the lives of so many others. We believe that it will also bring about significant improvements in the relationships you have with your own family and associates.

For ease in reading, the book was written as though I were the only writer; however the writing has been jointly shared by my wife and me. The experiences presented are a combination of ours and the collected experiences that others have shared with us along the way. We have incorporated them into the writing to assist in showing actual cases where these principles have been effectively used.

ACKNOWLEDGMENTS

I must acknowledge the continued belief and encouragement of my best friend, companion, and wife. Joy has always been there with me in whatever and wherever life has taken us. She has shared her compassion as well as her talents as a professional writer, poet, and lyricist. She has pushed me gently in the writing process, without which this book would have stayed inside of me.

I pay tribute to our parents, Lynne and Elese Lundberg and Clarence and Opal Saunders who taught and loved without interfering. I also acknowledge and appreciate the way our five children, Michael, Lynda, Carol, John, and Paul and their spouses, have shared many of their experiences with us.

My first therapist mentor was and is my oldest brother, Dr. Lynne Jay Lundberg. He has helped me by sharing his knowledge and love. His wife, Elaine, my brother Don and his wife Jonia, have always been supportive to both Joy and me as we have written and performed.

Our editor, Howard Allan Christy, has been extremely valuable, helpful, and encouraging. As we wrote the manuscript, there was a group of family, friends, and associates who read it and gave valuable critiques and suggestions: Janice Kapp Perry, Don and Jonia Lundberg, Lee Saunders, Lynne Christy, Mike and Gail Kraus, Dr. Tom and Marilou Meyers, Fern Cox, Ann Wakefield, Jan Godfrey, Joan Rollins and Shawna Powelson.

One other person I must acknowledge is Leo Weidner. He has been a unique blend of friend, neighbor, and coach. We have shared ideas and insights from each of our fields of endeavor. His critique of our manuscript has been extremely valuable. I have felt his belief and trust in me by his referring clients to me.

Last but not least are the many friends, clients, and seminar attendants, who have contributed their experiences and willingness to try these principles.

And now, thanks to you, the reader, for choosing "*I Don't Have To Make Everything All Better.*" I believe that by opening this book you will be opening the door to an exciting new time of lifted burdens—a lifetime filled with caring and loving relationships.

Gary Lundberg

Table Of Contents

————••••••————

Section One

This section will help you understand the six principles
needed to effectively walk emotionally with the
people you care about and empower
them to solve their own problems.

————••••••————

—••••—

Section Two

This section contains a wide variety of examples
that illustrate the practical application
of the principles explained in
Section One.

—••••—

Chapter Nine • How Validation Works With Adult Children 168

Chapter Ten • How Validation Works With A Spouse 195

Chapter Eleven • How Validation Works With Parents And Parents-In-Law 222

Introduction

————·••·•——————

Learning that I don't have the power to solve other people's problems, even those of my own family members, and that by validating their feelings appropriately I empower them to be their own problem solvers, has significantly increased the quality of my relationship with them.

Life is full of experiences that have emotions attached to them, and they can be positive or negative. When we are going through these emotions most of us want to be able to talk to someone who cares, someone who we care about. See if you can identify with this experience.

I had had an extremely hard day at the office. Nothing seemed to go right. I sat down with my close friend and wanted to just tell him what I had experienced. As I started to tell him, he would break in with what he thought I could have done or what I could now do to solve my problem. I didn't need this kind of help. Inside I felt like screaming, "Be quiet and listen to me. I need to tell someone what went on before I burst and I thought you really cared about me and would understand." I felt frustrated, ended the conversation quickly, and left feeling sad and hurt. (See Chapter Thirteen - *How Validation Works With Friends*)

The mother of a teenage girl told me of an incident when her daughter expressed her anger and dismay over how her friends were treating her.

My daughter said. "Mom, all they do is use me and treat me rude. They borrow my clothes, don't give them back when I want them, and when they give them back they're dirty." I knew the answer to her problem so I said, "Well, honey, the answer is simple. Just don't lend them your clothes and go get the ones they have and bring them home." She glared at me and said, "You just don't understand. You don't care. You never listen to me!" With that she ran out of the room. All I wanted to do was help her. (See Chapter Eight - *How Validation Works With Teenagers*)

In one form or another, incidents like these

have happened to me many times and probably you have also experienced them. Because I didn't know any different, I responded the same way to others. When I was the one giving the advice and the other person left looking sad, I thought, "I was only trying to help you out." I believed I could solve the other person's problem and make things all better with my advice and wise counsel. Yet, they left in a little bit of a huff much like I had done.

At one time in our married life, I felt like I didn't want to tell my wife my problems. She would give me advice and tell me what to do or she would try to interpret what I was feeling. When we talked this frustration out, I found out that I was doing the same thing to her. We both had the same justification which was, *we were wanting to help by solving each other's problem. After all, isn't this what spouses are for?* (See Chapter Ten - *How Validation Works With a Spouse*)

When we are on the giving end we forget how it feels to be on the receiving end. When someone starts telling us their problems we automatically shift into the solving mode or the defensive mode. Take the experience of a customer service representative:

The phone on my desk rang and I answered it. In a very loud voice the man said, "I hope you can help me because I have now talked to three other people and I want something done! My car has been in your lousy shop three times in the last two weeks for the same problem and it still isn't fixed!" I said, "Could you tell me what is wrong with it now?" "If I knew what was wrong with the #@*#@ car I would have fixed it myself," he said. I replied, "I'm sorry you are having such trouble." He broke in and said, "I'll say you're sorry. You are the sorriest bunch of people I know. Now what the @#$#@ are you going to do to fix my car." I found myself responding angrily, "Hey look mister, it's not my fault you car isn't fixed!!!" (See Chapter Fourteen - *How Validation Works On the Job*)

Figuring out how to respond to other people in a variety of situations is very difficult. Somehow we believe it is our moral responsibility to fix everything and everybody or we believe that everybody believes it is our moral responsibility to solve their problems. This is a terrible burden to carry around and often causes us to feel like jumping in a hole and dragging it in with us. What causes this shift into attempting to be everybody's problem solver?   Where did this obligation first start?

Most of us do not know when the idea of our having to take care of other people's problems began. One of my clients said, "It's just always been there. I somehow feel compelled to make other people all better." Other clients, friends and family members have made similar remarks. It seems that if someone they care about is having a hard time, it is up to them to find the solution. Here are a few of the remarks that are representative of the many I have heard over and over:

> "I must give off some kind of aura that says to other people that I can solve their problems, because even strangers tell me their problems."

> "All my life I was told to take care of my younger brothers and sisters—that they were my responsibility. If they argued, I was to handle the problem and stop the argument. If they were hungry, I was to feed them. I was to change the diapers, do the family laundry and keep the house clean. Whatever *I* wanted to do was never a consideration. Though that was a long time ago, I still feel responsible for solving all their problems and meeting all their needs."

> "My children have suffered so much because of the divorce, I must make it easier for them so they won't have to suffer any more. My new spouse will just have to understand."

"Every time my wife tells me some problem, I feel it is my responsibility to solve it. She seems to be saying, 'Well, what are you going to do about it?' "

I don't have the power to solve other people's problems. By validating their feelings appropriately I empower them to be their own problem solver.

"I have always known I must keep everybody cheered up. It's my job to be positive and make them happy."

"My son and his wife are struggling financially and they complain about their struggles every time we are together. So what am I supposed to do? Send them money so they won't have to struggle? I keep trying to tell them they don't have it so bad."

Did any of these remarks have a familiar ring to you? In the past I have had some of these same feelings myself and made many mistakes because I didn't understand the importance of validating the feelings of others, nor did I know how. I thought it was my duty to solve the problems, expressed or unexpressed, of my family, friends and others I knew. Learning that I don't have the power to solve other people's problems, even those of my own family members, and that by validating their feelings appropriately I empower them to be their own problem solvers, has significantly increased the quality of our relationships. In addition, I have witnessed a far greater measure of success in their personal lives, and an increase in the quality of my own.

Knowing the significance of what can happen in the life of anyone using these principles has inspired a desire within me to share them with my clients, as well as those attending our seminars, and others at every appropriate opportunity. As I have shared them, and people

> *Validation is not a cure all. It is a way to let people close to you carry their own responsibilities while helping them feel loved by you to a far greater degree.*

begin to understand the process of validation and how it empowers others to more effectively solve their own problems, they want to know more. It is rewarding to see the excitement in their eyes as they learn how to be a true listener and friend to family members and other associates.

Validation is not a new concept. However, many do not seem to understand how simple it is and the positive effect it can have in their relationships with others. Some may already be using it to some degree, but fall short of the total application. Through the information in this book we illustrate the concepts and practice of validation in such a way that there is no doubt as to how you can use it effectively—even automatically—every day of your life. By so doing, you can find greater fulfillment, peace and joy in all your relationships.

Validation is not a cure all. It is a way to get some relief from carrying burdens that are not yours. It is a way to let people close to you carry their own responsibilities, while helping them feel loved by you to a far greater degree. You may not believe this statement, and many don't at first, but it is true: You really do not have to make it all better.

The first six chapters (Section One) explain the principles and concepts relating to validation. By carefully reading these chapters you will have a basic understanding of the importance of them and how to use them. These are the fundamentals that will help you fully understand the applications and examples given in the balance of the book.

The last eight chapters (Section Two) show how validation can be, and has been, effectively used in various real-life situations. Most of these examples have come to us from people who have learned the concepts and have used them in their own lives. They were willing to share them so others could see how effective the concepts can be. Some of the examples show the adverse effects of their misuse, making the value of validation even more obvious. You will likely see yourself in many of the situations. They are everyday, where-the-rubber-meets-the-road kinds of experiences that each of us meet head-on at one time or another. As you read, you will likely have some "Ah ha. . . now I get it" experiences.

Of course, the examples cited in this book do not cover every situation you may experience in using validation. They are rather a sampling to stimulate your thinking. It may seem that the same validating phrases are being repeated. It is because they are easy to use and when received, feel so good. Use them for similarities you may face and look for ways they may help you handle the many situations that are uniquely yours.

Some of the ideas covered in this book may seem simplistic, yet they do work when used simply. Do not discount the simplicity of them. Give validation an honest try in your own life before making a judgment. It does work.

We have written this book in an easy-to-read style so that all readers will be able to comfortably grasp the concepts presented and enjoy the process of learning.

Section One

This section will help you understand the six principles needed to effectively walk emotionally with the people you care about and empower them to solve their own problems.

Chapter One

─────── ··•·· ───────

Principle 1
Be An Effective Validator

LET ME FEEL WHAT I AM FEELING

Everyday throughout the world, in nearly every situation, people are constantly trying to express their feelings to someone. Consider the following examples:

- It is a cold winter morning as you awaken your child. "I don't want to get up. It's too cold," the child says. You reply, "It's not that cold. You just need to get up and get your blood going and you'll be just fine."

- You come home from work and dinner isn't ready. Your wife, a stay-at-home mother of three, says, "I don't feel like cooking dinner tonight. I get tired of it day in and day out." You come back with, "You think you've got it hard. You just don't know how lucky you are. You get to stay home. I have to go to work every day."

• Your athletic son comes home looking sad and dejected. "I didn't make the starting lineup," he says. You reply, "Well, just keep doing your best and you'll make it eventually."

> *The universal need within each of us — I am of worth, my feelings matter, and someone really cares about me.*

• Your young married daughter complains to you, "Married life is hard. There's just not enough money for anything extra." And you reply, "Honey, you don't know what hard times are. When your dad and I were newlyweds we . . ."

• Your friend, a cement finisher, says, "Man, it's hot out here. Sometimes I feel like a piece of chicken in a frying pan." And you, a cement truck driver, reply, "You oughta be sitting in this truck, then you'd know what hot is."

Unfortunately, too many of us respond as those in the above examples. We fail to recognize the universal need within each of us to truly believe that *I am of worth, my feelings matter, and someone really cares about me.* This need begins to be fulfilled when people are able to recognize and express their own personal feelings.

The identifying of one's own feelings is difficult for some people, especially males. Also there are others, male and female, who have not been allowed to express what is going on inside of themselves. Sadly, during their growing up period, many are told by their parents, teachers, or friends that they have no right to feel the way they are feeling. One client said that every time he tried to talk about his feelings his parents would say, "Children should be seen and not heard. So be quiet and go play." He said, "I learned it was not safe to express my feelings or needs. If I did, they were used against me to embarrass me." He went on, " Sometimes when other adults were visiting our home one of my parents would say, 'Do you know what our son said?' Then they would repeat what I had said and make fun of it."

Another client said every time she started to talk about her feelings, she was told the feelings she expressed were not right and she shouldn't feel that way. Her parents would then tell her what feelings were right for the situation.

On a national talk show, two women were discussing their feelings concerning their childhood.

They were telling their mother they often felt of little worth due to the way she responded to them as they expressed their feelings to her when they were children. One daughter said when she had shared a feeling with her mother, her mother had replied, "You shouldn't feel that way, you should feel this way." The daughter said, "I went away believing I didn't matter as a person and my feelings didn't count for anything." The daughter looked at her mother there on the show and, in tears, said, "All I needed to hear was that you understood what I was feeling. Then I would have gone away feeling like I was worth something."

These scenes happen over and over everyday throughout the world. As I have seen the sorrow and lack of self-esteem this causes, I have wished to help people understand the principle of validation. It is based on the personal understanding that I am acceptable just the way I am, and you are acceptable the way you are. Too many people believe, "I am acceptable and you will be acceptable when you believe, see, feel, and talk like I do."

All of us want to be listened to and understood. We want to be appreciated for who we are individually. We need to be heard completely and not judged, corrected, or advised. When those who are meaningful in our life will not take the time to hear us out by genuinely listening, we experience a profound negative effect much like the two examples above.

In many families, tradition has dictated that children, no matter the age, are to be seen and not heard. Parents are the possessors of all knowledge and wisdom. Children remain children until the parents die, and until that time the children are to look to the parents as all-wise and all-knowing. They, the children, are to accept and follow the parents' counsel without question. These are extreme statements and yet, to some degree, they exist in most families. This attitude is stifling to personal growth and does not show respect and understanding.

There is a parallel in interpersonal relationships. Much like the "all-knowing" parent, most of us want to be looked to as being wise. Most of us want to be able to help others solve their problems. We, both men and women, automatically think when someone brings up a problem, we must immediately solve it for them. In fact, as the person is sharing their problem with us, rather than listening fully, our minds are racing with solutions for them and we can hardly wait for them to stop talking so we can tell them what they should be doing about it. We care about them and we think it is our responsibility to help them in this way. This places a strain on communication between friends and family members that need not be there.

Feeling the need to always have the answer also exists in some business situations. If I am the owner, or supervisor, I must have the answer for all needs or problems. Sometimes this is necessary when it comes to policy or final approval, but in problem solving, this can be a terrible burden for one to carry. Even some business owners believe workers are to do what they are told and leave the thinking up to the boss. Companies with this philosophy have been meeting harder times than those with a more listening-ear approach. New ideas, which often come through the process of validation, are vital to success.

> *Validation is the act, process, or instance of confirming or corroborating the meaningfulness and relevance of what another person (or self) is feeling.*

DEFINING VALIDATION

At this point it may help by defining validation from the dictionary.[1] Starting with the first part of the word, "valid," some of its meanings are "well grounded or justifiable; being at once relevant and meaningful; appropriate to the end in view." Adding the second part of the word to make "validate," two of its meanings are "to confirm the validity of," and "to support or corroborate on a sound basis." Taking the whole word, "validation," one of its meanings is "an act, process, or instance of validating."

Using a combination of these definitions, validation then is the act, process, or instance of confirming or corroborating the meaningfulness and relevance of what another person (or self) is feeling. To put it more simply, it is being able to empathetically listen and understand another person's point of view without having to change it.

Another way of stating this is that validation is the ability to walk with another person emotionally without trying to change his or her direction. Robert Bly, an American poet and instigator of the men's movement called "A Gathering of Men," was interviewed by TV commentator Bill Moyers on a PBS television show. He said, "In a conversation there are little turns, you can turn up or down. When one says, 'I lost my brother five years ago,' at that point, you can say, 'Well, we all lose our brothers,' or you can touch a hand, or you can go into the part of you that's lost a brother. You can follow the grief downward in this way." When we walk with another emotionally, we treat that person gently, kindly, and respectfully. In other words, we treat him like we would like to be treated. When a person is allowed to follow his emotions down as far as he needs to go with someone

> *When a person is allowed to follow the emotions down as far as he needs to go with someone walking beside him emotionally, then he will bring himself back up.*

walking beside him emotionally, then he will bring himself back up.

[Note: At this point, I must acknowledge that there is a wide range of emotional problems. Some will only respond to medication, some will only respond to counseling, while there are others that will require a combination of both medication and counseling. One wide spread problem is clinical depression. This is a condition of deep, ongoing depression that needs medical attention. When someone is diagnosed as having clinical depression, that person may need to have medication to balance out their physiological system. In most cases, medication alone will not solve the problem, but it will allow the chance to develop coping mechanisms from which solutions are possible. Validation helps in the process of developing these solutions.]

WHAT ABOUT POSITIVE MENTAL ATTITUDE?

There is a philosophy taught called Positive Mental Attitude (PMA). We are told many ills are cured with PMA. We are taught to always look on the bright side of life. Therefore, the way to help another is to tell the bright side, give people a big dose of PMA no matter how they are feeling. While this may be appropriate at a certain point, we each need to get there in our own time. When someone tells you to "look on the bright side," inside you may be saying,

"But you just don't understand. Right now I am not able to see the bright side."

Suppose you have just been diagnosed with an early stage of cancer. You call a friend to tell her the terrible news, adding, "I'm really scared. People die of cancer every day." How would you feel at this point if your friend said, "Cheer up. They caught it early. You probably don't have anything to worry about." How sensitive is your friend to what you are feeling? What is it that you need from her at this moment? Is this the time you need to hear a PMA? How much better might you feel if your friend said, "Oh, I am so sorry to hear about that." Then follow up with a question such as, "How did you find out about it?" or "What did the doctor say?" This then allows you to talk about it, telling your friend more about the problem, what's worrying you, how serious it might be, and what the doctor is recommending.

There is an inherent desire and need directing each of us to the bright side of our own life. Our basic nature pushes us to see new possibilities or solutions. However, there is also a need to be able to acknowledge our own feelings *before* we can see the bright side, and to know it is permissible to feel what we are feeling. Once we deal with the emotion, then we are ready to go forward with a more positive attitude. And we are much more able to discover the bright side as we emotionally walk with each other.

A client of mine, I'll call him John, shared that he was glad to have learned how to let a person go to the emotional depths necessary without using PMA's or trying to change him. His thirteen year-old son came in one day and said, "I hate Jim." Usually John's parental side would react by telling the son not to use the word hate because he didn't really mean "hate." Instead of standing in his son's way with such an invalidating statement, he used the small powerful word "Oh" (a simple statement, not a question). Then his son went on to share his story of what had been said and done. John said, "There are hooks my son knows how to use to get me emotionally involved and reactive." He explained, "My son said, 'Jim told me his parents talk about you and say you earn more money than you know what to do with and you waste it.' I dodged this by saying, 'That must have hurt you when they talked about your dad that way." The son said, "Yeah, I wanted to kill him." This too, was a hook and John dodged it by saying, "I can see you are really angry." The son said that he really was angry and then began to pour out his feelings. John said, "All I did was listen and validate his feelings. His anger subsided and he went out to play." He stated that the more he listened and walked with his son the more open his son became. As a result the son was able to let the anger go and their relationship has grown to be more peaceful than it has ever been.

> *Because you are comfortable with yourself and your own value system, you can listen and learn, and accept or reject what other people say or do.*

VALIDATION BEGINS WITH SELF

Validation is based on a strong belief in yourself and your own value system. This means you do not have to receive direction from outside yourself concerning the values, beliefs, and principles that direct your life. In other words, you are comfortable with yourself. If someone believes differently than you do, you do not feel threatened. It also means if someone behaves differently than you do, you do not need to change your beliefs or behaviors to fit theirs.

Who you are is who you choose to be. When you have a strong belief system, based on what you have learned, studied, and experienced, then you have developed a model of life which is used to evaluate everything you come in contact with. You can hear another viewpoint and can evaluate it on its merits and even ask the question, "Is this right for me?" Because you are comfortable with yourself and your own value system, you can listen and learn, and accept or reject what other people say or do.

VALIDATION IS NOT MANIPULATION

Each of us must determine what our view of humankind is. If we believe that people are there for us to control and manipulate at will, then validation will not work for us. If our view is a basic faith in the natural goodness of people, then validation will work for us. I believe most people are good and have an inborn desire pulling them toward a higher plane of existence. Most people desire to do right, to help others, and to lift mankind. This belief is supported by the many innumerable acts of human kindness rendered by those who have nothing to gain by offering aid to others who suffer. For instance, people appear, almost from nowhere, to help victims of disasters. These acts are not limited to a specific location in the world—they happen everywhere. Food and shelter is shared, medical care is rendered, comfort given to those who are saddened or grieving, and talents are shared to lift others' spirits. There are countless numbers of talented performers who visit hospitals and rest homes just to lighten the load of others. Some do it for publicity, but most do it simply because they care.

> *Offering help leaves responsibility with the appropriate person.*

It is important to ask ourselves: What is my motivation for what I do? What is my life paradigm (view) based on? If I give help to another person for what I think I can get in return, then maybe I am like a puppet on a string. Do I feel manipulated much of the time? If so, then maybe I need to reconsider how I value myself and look at my belief in my own value system. If I see others as manipulative, maybe I need to look at what I do to see if I am manipulating others.

Having a strong comfortable belief in my value system means I have the right to choose and must take responsibility for my thoughts, beliefs, and actions. This also means I believe other people have the same right and responsibility. Sometimes, in our desire to help others, we take away their responsibility. Offering help leaves responsibility with the appropriate person. This is done with questions like; "How can I help you?" "Is there something I can do to help?" "Would it help if I did such and such?"

These questions leave the responsibility for what is done with the person you are offering to help. Again comes the question as to your motivation

> *Personal boundaries are your value system in action.*

for offering help. Is it: Do I genuinely care about this person and want to help? Do I offer help so that when I need something I cannot be turned down by this person? Do I help others so people will see what I am doing and will give me recognition? I am not naive enough to think everything is done with a single motivation. Sometimes there is a combination. However, everything comes back to your overall personal motivation, which is based on your value system. A value system is what determines a person's boundaries.

PERSONAL BOUNDARIES DO NOT HAVE TO CHANGE

Personal boundaries define you as an individual. They are statements of what you will or won't do, what you like and don't like, how far you will or won't go, how close someone can get to you or how close you will get to another person. There are many other statements that describe boundaries. To sum it up, they are your value system in action. When you are comfortable with your value system, you can state your boundaries without having to defend or justify them. I believe boundaries need to have four attributes. They need to be (1) Kind (2) Gentle (3) Respectful, and (4) Firm. There is no need to yell, defend, or justify what they are. They are simply yours.

When you attempt to understand another person, that does not change your values or boundaries. All you are doing is walking beside another to try to understand. For instance, as someone goes through the process of deciding on an action, he might make a statement like, "I would like to punch the person right in the nose." Your value system says, "I could not physically harm another." However, have you ever felt like you would *like* to punch someone, and because of your value system, you wouldn't do it? If you have felt that way, you can say, "I can understand that feeling." All you are doing is UNDERSTANDING. You do not have to agree or condone the action.

Understanding the feelings of another allows that person to freely express feelings and to effectively process internal struggles. If the feeling is validated, usually that person will come up with a responsible conclusion and action. The ability to indulge in a small personal catharsis by even contemplating something as crazy as an old fashioned punch in the nose, helps the person come up with a good solution. I have watched this happen time and time again in my office. Some silly or crazy action is considered and there is an emotional reaction within the person, followed by the statement, "I really couldn't do that. But it felt good for a moment." Then comes the process, as explained in the next chapter, of helping the person find his own best solution, NOT YOUR SOLUTION—HIS. Throughout this process no one needs to change his value system or actions.

THE UNIVERSAL NEED

The key to making validation a habit is to remember that every person you see has the universal need to believe inside themselves that: I AM OF WORTH, MY FEELINGS MATTER, AND SOMEONE REALLY CARES ABOUT ME. It would be well to memorize this statement so you can recall it whenever anyone begins to share personal feelings with you. It is through your recognition of their worth that others will feel loved by you and empowered to solve their own problems.

Chapter Two

Principle 2
Leave The Responsibility Where It Belongs

THE UNDERLYING PRINCIPLE

When you validate others, you are then free of the burden of needing to solve the other person's problems, allowing you to give your full attention to what is being said. Many people do not understand the important underlying principle this statement is based on. It is:

I DO NOT HAVE THE POWER TO MAKE ANYTHING ALL BETTER FOR ANYONE ELSE.

(Note: Before the word *anything* causes you a feeling of despair and worthlessness, please read on.)

When I have presented this principle at seminars, I have asked the audience to vote as to whether or not they believe the statement. Usually the vote is split fairly evenly between "do believe," "don't believe," and "don't know." One woman said out loud, "Then, what good are we if we can't make things all better?" The following examples may help make the principle more clearly understood.

(1) If someone breaks an arm or some other bone, no matter how much skill a doctor has, can he make the broken bone all better?

(2) Your friend's company is involved in major layoffs and he loses his job. He's devastated and pours out his frustrations to you. Can you make it all better? Can you save his job?

(3) Someone loses a loved one through death. Can you bring the loved one back and make it all better?

> *We get power mixed up with desire.*

No matter how hard one may try, past events cannot be changed. When sickness comes, an accident happens, a bone is broken, hurtful things are said, a divorce takes place, a loved one dies, a friend moves away, someone is abused, a natural disaster occurs, war comes and people are killed or maimed—none of these can be changed after they have happened. We all wish these events had not happened and we would like to be able to change them. This is a normal desire.

POWER AND DESIRE

The problem is that we get *power* mixed up with *desire*. When audiences are asked how many *want* to make it all better for someone they care about, the vote is unanimous. It seems there is a universal inborn desire to help someone in trouble and to be the one able to solve the other person's problem. The confusion and frustration come from not knowing what to do and how far to go. We all have a desire to help each other in times of stress, tragedy, or disaster. The amount of good that is done by people caring for other people cannot be measured. The examples of people helping others during the aftermath of hurricanes, floods, fires, earthquakes, and accidents would fill volumes. Burdens are lifted when help is given; however, this does not make the problem all better. Each person must face the problem squarely and deal with the event and its losses. Only the person can heal himself.

I remember when, as a little child, I cut my finger. It hurt and I went crying to my mother. She cleaned it, put some disinfectant on it (which usually hurt more), bandaged it, and then kissed it and said,

"Now it is all better." In reality, the cut was not all better. It still hurt and if bumped, it would bleed. But something was different. What was it? I seemed to feel better and I was happy to go out to show my playmates the new bandage and then to resume playing. What changed? The change happened in my mind because I knew someone understood my need and offered the help that was possible.

So the complete statement is:

I *DO NOT HAVE THE POWER TO MAKE ANYTHING ALL BETTER FOR ANYONE ELSE.   I CAN OFFER MY HELP, BUT I CANNOT MAKE IT ALL BETTER.*

OFFERING HELP

Offering help can be loving and respectful when it is done in the right way. As in the case of the broken bone, the doctor can set the broken bone and relieve pain. However, the healing takes time and happens within the person. Many needs are not as easily defined as a broken bone. To assess needs, you could ask questions like the following: How can I help you? Is there something I can do for you? Is there something you need? Is there something you would like me to do? I would like to be of help, what can I do? Would it help if I did such and such? These are

> "Should" and
> "Ought"—two words
> that strongly imply
> obligation and
> expectation rather than
> choice.

a few suggestions and there are many other ways to phrase questions that offer help. They leave the responsibility for what needs to be done with the person who has the problem.

It is often helpful to suggest something you can do. There is a period of confusion after traumatic events and the needs may be difficult to express. For instance, a family recently lost their son, and neighbors brought in food to help ease the burden of fixing meals. One neighbor came in saying he would like to shine all the family's shoes to help them prepare for the funeral. As he shined the shoes, he began talking with one of the parents and listened as the parent talked of the sadness experienced.

Too often help is offered in a way that tries to take away the other person's responsibility. Sometimes this is done under the cloak of advice. Advice comes with the best of intentions and usually has two key words with it, "should" and "ought." These two words strongly imply obligation and expectation rather than choice. For example, if you're having a difficult time with your boss at work, and you verbalize your frustration, someone might respond with, "You should be forceful and tell your boss just where you stand." The person receiving the advice may be thinking, "You don't know my boss. If I forcefully stand up to him, I may lose my job. I just needed to talk about this to someone." (See Chapter Fourteen—*How Validation Works With Friends*)

How about the parent who is sharing her frustration over her child's behavior? People have all kinds of "shoulds" and "oughts" they love to give regarding children—especially those who do not have children. For example, "You should spank your child" or "You ought to ground him for a week." Then if you don't do what they said, you may hear, "Well, I told you what you should have done."

MAKING DECISIONS FOR OTHERS

Along with giving advice, sometimes we unintentionally make decisions for others without asking them first. See if you can find yourself in any of the following examples:

(1) *Setting up a job interview for a friend without first consulting with the friend.* This may make the friend feel obligated to be there for a job he is not interested in or trained for. In this situation the friend may think you consider him ungrateful if he does not respond, or, if he gets the job and it does not work out well for him, he may consider you responsible for pushing him into something he didn't want.

(2) *Taking a phone call and making a commitment for someone who is not there.* When the person returns he is informed, "I told him you would call him" or " I told them you would be right over as soon as you arrived." Here one person makes a commitment for another person rather than saying "I will give him the message."

(3) *Ordering someone else's meal before they arrive* at *the restaurant.* Here again a commitment is made without asking.

When help is offered, it is best received when the other person's choice or responsibility is recognized and not taken away.

RESPONSIBILITY FOR THE PROBLEM

Did you ever play the children's game of "Hot Potato"? The idea of the game is to not end up with the object representing the "Hot Potato" when the music stops. Problems are much like the hot potatoes. The object is to pass them on as quickly as possible. It is rough being the one to end up with the responsibility for a problem, even if the problem is your own.

As with anything that is uncomfortable, most

people want to get rid of it as soon as possible. I don't know of anyone who wants to keep a problem. So, if I have a problem, what do I do with it? Maybe I don't want to solve it myself; maybe I don't know how to solve it; maybe the solution is too hard; maybe I believe you can do it faster, better, or easier; or maybe I just want to pass it on. One solution is to look for the hero waiting to be my rescuer—YOU!

This may sound as though I believe people with problems are looking to "hook someone" by any devious means available. There are some people in the world who may do that, but I believe most people try to solve their own problems first, then become desperate for help. It is during this time of desperation that people look for someone to relieve them of their problems.

The desire to be liked, be admired for getting things done, or be able to solve problems can make us the vulnerable one who ends up with the "Hot Potato." However, I don't believe we set out to be responsible for the other person's problems, but many times we realize too late that the problem is now in our hands. How does this happen?

In helping my clients understand how this works, I have used a fictitious scenario that almost always manipulates the client into taking full or partial responsibility for my problem. After they have accepted my problem and we talk it over, they admit that this has happened to them the same way many times. And they admit they end up feeling burdened and frustrated. Here is the scenario:

> I say: "Jill, you and I have been friends for many years and I feel like I can talk to you about a problem. My wife and I have been having problems with our daughter, Tami. We just can't seem to talk with her without arguing and we are not close anymore. I am almost at my wits end and am desperate for some help."
>
> Jill usually says: "Oh, I am sorry to hear that. What would you like me to do?"

(During my professional training, I was warned that it is easy to get sidetracked from the main issue at hand and we must not get so involved in the content of the story or problem that the process of what is going on is missed. Everyone likes a good story and when it involves a friend, one can get emotionally tied up in the story. We use key phrases in passing responsibility to another person, and emotions sometimes cause us to miss these phrases. As the role playing continues, see if you can identify those phrases.)

> I say: "I know how you relate well to others, and I think Tami would relate to you. She needs a friend. Would you be her

friend?"

Jill usually says: "Well, I think I can do that."

I say: "Oh, thank you very much. That takes a load off of my mind. I hope you'll call her soon."

Now I can feel some relief knowing my problem is now in Jill's hands. Jill stands there with a burdened feeling, thinking, "Now what do I do?" She has the "Hot Potato."

What is it that causes the burdened feeling when all Jill wants to do is help? The burden comes from Jill accepting a problem that is not adequately defined. What did I mean by asking her to "be Tami's friend?" She may be wondering, "What exactly did he have in mind and how can I be a friend to a much younger person? Am I supposed to go out with her? Do I invite her over to my home? Does he think she is going to move in with me?" Jill does not know what I expect of her. Until Jill can view the problem through my eyes or as close to that as possible, then the problem is as big as the whole world. The bounds and the expectations are all unknown to Jill.

In the next interchange, Jill tries to get more information but is outmaneuvered with an almost irrefutable passing of the "Hot Potato" once again.

> *Always remember where the responsibility for the problem belongs.*

Jill says: "Well, I am willing to make an effort to be Tami's friend. How do you see me doing that?"

I reply: "We have been praying for help and your name kept coming to us. Because your name came to us, I am sure you will know just what to do. Thanks so much for doing this."

Jill sits there thinking, "Oh dear, how can I argue with, or even question, God?"

Always remember where the responsibility for the problem belongs. If you do that, then you can continue to ask questions until what is needed is within the bounds you can handle. You do not need to argue with God. How about saying something like, "I'm really complimented that God feels I can help. However, I need some more information as to what you think can be done for your daughter." Now comes the time for questions using how, what, where, and when (See "The Art of Questioning" in the next chapter).

Throughout the scenario, were you able to pick out any of the phrases used to pass on responsibility? Some of the ones I used were:

"You and I have been friends for many years."

"I feel I can talk to you about a problem."
"I'm at my wits end and desperate."
"I know how well you relate to others."
"We have been praying . . . and your name."
"Because your name came to us, you'll know what to do."

Taken separately they seem all right; however, I have carefully put them together to pass on the responsibility. They may appear to be manipulative flattery but most people do not use them with cunning forethought.

There are many variations that people use to get someone to accept a problem. Our nine-year-old daughter came into the room where we were sitting with our two older boys, and said, "Mom, is there any handsome, strong young man around that could move my dresser out so I can get my comb that fell behind it?" Nobody had to say anything further because two boys were rushing down the hall to prove who was the handsome strong young man.

Other phrases used are:

"You are much better (or smarter, wiser, more talented, quicker, stronger, more experienced, etc.) at it than I am."
"I just don't know what to do."
"You are such a good friend."

The above examples are only a small sample of phrases that can hook you. Some of these same phrases used in the proper context could be genuine compliments. Take the compliment at face value and don't get hooked into taking someone else's responsibility.

IF I OFFER HELP AM I STUCK?

Offering help to another person is an act of kindness when it is motivated by genuine caring. It does not need to change your boundaries. Think about the following scenario and the commentary with each interchange. (Please do not get too involved with the story and lose the process of what is happening with the listener.)

Situation: Your neighbor is crying and looking despondent. You sit down and listen to the story. She is having trouble with her son. He is sullen, has no friends, and lacks self-esteem. As you listen and validate, the full story unfolds. Finally, she says, "I don't know what to do."

Now you use the validating question, "What would you like to do?" She says, "I would like to ship him to Siberia!" Can you understand that feeling? If so, say so! "I think

I can understand that feeling." Then she might say, with a laugh, "Yeah, but I don't have a one-way ticket! I am really at a loss as to what to do with him."

Because you genuinely care about your friend, you offer help by saying, "Is there any way I can help? She may say, "The only thing we have come up with is to buy him some clothes that are more stylish, but we don't have any money. It would help if you gave us some money to buy him the clothes."

[Note: I have used money as a metaphor for anything you might not be able to respond to. For example, the mother might want to have her son come live with you, or to have you be the one to discipline him, or to have you be the son's full-time home school teacher, etc. There are many requests that could fit in this category. If you have felt overwhelmed by a request made of you, then the following suggestions may help you handle situations in the future.]

At this point in the conversation you might respond with an impatient, "How could you ask such a thing? You know we are not made of money. He is your responsibility and not mine. Anyway, I don't believe in giving anyone money. I can't believe you would ask this." This response indicates discomfort with self, with values, with financial position, and a tendency to be offended.

Suppose your value system is as stated above and you don't believe in giving others money and your financial position is limited. Remember your position in life and your value system is okay. How about a reply like, "I wish I could do that, but I'm not in a position to do so. Is there any other way I can help you?" This indicates personal comfort with your values and life position, and the confidence not to be easily offended. It also says you care about her and are willing to help in other ways that are appropriate. You do not need to change your values or behavior when offering help.

Even if there is an angry response, you do not need to change your beliefs or values. For instance, she may say, "I thought you were my friend, and you offered to help me. Some friend you turned out to be." This could evoke guilt feelings and the feeling of being manipulated if you let it. Instead, stand firm and reply, "I *am* your friend and would like to help in areas that I am able. Is there some other way I

> *When you offer help you must attempt to see through the eyes of the other person what is needed and wanted. The only way to do this is to ask nonthreatening questions.*

can help you?"

When anyone offers help there are always limitations as to what one can do. There are many questions that can be asked to determine needs and to narrow these down to something you can handle. For instance, you could respond with one of the following: "What else is going on with your son?", "What can you see that could be done?" She may say, "Could you talk to my son?" Then you could ask, "What needs to be talked about?" Or "What points are you trying to get across to him?" Or "How would you like that said?"

When you offer help you must attempt to see through the eyes of the other person to determine what is needed and wanted. The only way to do this is to ask nonthreatening questions that are designed to gather information. The questions must not appear to pass judgment.

Chapter Three

Principle 3
Acknowledge Emotions

THE FOUR BASIC EMOTIONS

In my work with troubled teens at a regional medical center, I became aware that many of those teens could not recognize what was going on inside themselves. By watching their eyes, I could see that they were experiencing some emotion, yet, when asked what they were feeling they would reply they did not know. Since that time, I have seen many clients of all ages who could not verbalize what they were feeling. This confirmed that they had learned one or a combination of four emotionally misleading concepts: (1) It is not safe to express feelings, (2) It is not okay to believe what I am feeling; rather, look to someone else to tell me what to feel, (3) It doesn't matter what I feel, and (4) Emotions are bad.

Dr. Jay Lundberg (my brother, who is also a marriage and family therapist), came up with a short menu of feelings I like to use in my practice. He has identified the four basic emotions as: *Mad, Glad, Sad,* and *Afraid.* Each of these emotions has many other names or descriptions, but this simplified list is a good place to start.

It is important to recognize that you may have more than one emotion at a time. Some may say they have a feeling of frustration or confusion. This generally comes when more than one emotion is felt at the same time. By examining each part of the frustration, you may be able to understand yourself better. These emotions can be broken down into a combination of the basic four, that is, mad and sad, or afraid and mad, or glad and sad, and so on. The following are examples of situations that elicit more than one emotion:

Mad, Sad, and Glad - A promotion at work is given to another person and you are feeling *mad* that you didn't get the promotion and *sad* that you weren't recognized for your hard

> *Nobody needs permission to feel, because the emotions are there. The sooner we recognize them the better off we are.*

work. And to complicate it further, you are trying to feel *glad* for the other person.

Glad and Sad - When one of our sons and his wife decided to move to a city a thousand miles away for a new job opportunity, we were *glad* he would have the chance for a better job and *sad* that they would be so far away.

Mad, Glad, Sad, and Afraid - I had an automobile accident some years ago where I turned left at a busy intersection and didn't see a small car approaching. After the dust settled, I felt *mad* at myself for not seeing the car, *sad* that I caused the accident, *glad* that nobody was hurt, and *afraid* of what would have happened if we had been a few feet further into the intersection.

> *In order to control the negative effects emotions can have on our bodies it becomes important to be able to recognize them.*

The important thing to know is we all have emotions and we can feel more than one emotion at a time. They are there whether we recognize them or not. Nobody needs to wait for permission to feel, because the emotions are there. The sooner we recognize them, the better off we are.

EMOTIONS CAN AFFECT OUR PHYSICAL WELL-BEING

Emotions play an important role in our physical well-being. In order to control the negative effects emotions can have on our bodies it becomes important to be able to recognize them. Through my own experience I have come to believe that emotions manifest themselves in different places in our bodies.

Let's first consider *mad.* Think about a time when you were extremely angry—one of those door-slamming, teeth-clenching mads. You felt a great big knot. Where was it? When asked this question at my seminars everyone says, "In the stomach." I then ask, "What happens to people who have a lot of unresolved anger?" Without exception, their response is, "Ulcers." I concur. Thus, it is a safe assumption that anger often manifests itself in the area of the stomach. One of my clients who was angry over unfair treatment by his employer experienced severe abdominal pain. His doctor ran tests on him and found he had ulcers. Another client said she had experienced unresolved anger for several years and, as a result, had had two-thirds of her stomach removed due to ulcers. If ulcers are caused by a bacteria, as some research indicates, it is probable that our emotions suppress our ability to fight the bacteria, allowing the ulcer to grow.

What about *afraid?* Remember a time when you were all alone at night. It was very quiet as you sat there reading and suddenly you heard a strange noise in the other room. Fearing someone was trying to break in, you picked up the fireplace tool and carefully moved toward the other room to investigate.

What physical effects were you feeling? A person in this situation will usually feel a restriction in their breathing; a shortness of breath with a tightness in the chest area. Another client of mine was so bound up in fear that she carried an atomizer with her to aid in loosening up her breathing.

What about *sad*? I personally remember a time years ago when I felt deep sorrow over a tragedy that had struck a close friend of mine. I could hardly bear to see the agony he was going through. The feeling I felt was an actual pain in the area of my heart. People who experience extreme sorrow do suffer what feels like a "broken heart." If sorrow is not addressed and dealt with appropriately it can eventually take a dramatic toll on our physical well-being.

What about *glad*? We have all heard the phrases "a happy heart" and "a glad heart." It seems that gladness has the power to kick sadness out of its place in our heart and take over, spreading throughout our entire body. It is the great healing emotion. When we feel happy inside, natural endorphins are released from our brain and bring about pleasant sensations of well-being.

> *Too often we unintentionally teach our children and others not to trust their own feelings.*

I mention these emotions in a simplified form to help you see the powerful effect they have on our bodies. There is increasing scientific evidence that unresolved negative emotions depress our immune systems and cause us to be more vulnerable to many diseases and physical ailments. Therefore, it is important for us to recognize and appropriately deal with our own emotions *and* the emotions of others. When we fail to allow others to feel what they are feeling we may inadvertently complicate their lives, mentally and physically.

UNINTENTIONAL TEACHING

Too often we unintentionally teach our children and others not to trust their own feelings. This is done with small statements that carry far greater impact than we realize. The following two examples show everyday situations that I confess I have been guilty of and have observed in others as well.

Example 1:

Mothers, remember one of the times when you decided to fix a special meal. The menu consisted of all the trimmings—meat, potatoes, gravy, vegetables, salad, dressing, rolls, butter, punch, and dessert. You painstakingly placed everything on the table and called the family. Then came the thundering hoofbeats of the hungry hoard. They surrounded the table, perhaps paused momentarily for a quick blessing on the food, and then inhaled the entire meal.

There is something magical that happens to a teenage boy about thirty minutes later. If you are lucky it may wait to forty-five minutes or if unlucky it may happen in twenty minutes. He strolls into the kitchen and says, "I'm hungry." Be honest now, what is your usual reply? I have found myself saying, "You just ate. You can't be hungry." In the many presentations I have given, this seems to be the reply given by most people.

Example 2:

You are sitting in the living room when the front door bursts open and in runs your daughter with her fists clenched tightly, her jaw set firmly, and she hollers, "I hate Miss Smith!" Again, what is your usual reply? It seems the common response is, "Dear, you don't really hate anybody." Sometimes we then use the big weapon that carries with it a real guilt trip, "God wouldn't want you to hate."

The initial reaction is the beginning of an argument with the boy saying, "I *am* hungry" and the girl saying "I *do* hate her." There is a process going on inside of these two teenagers that they may not be aware of. For the boy the subconscious thought process is something like this: "Mom (or Dad) says I am not hungry, so how come it feels like the front side of my stomach is eating the back side? I interpret this as hunger. However, my parents say I'm not hungry and they would not lie to me, so my feelings must be lying to me." The daughter's subconscious process is much the same, "Mom (or Dad) says I don't hate, yet how come I have these clenched fists and tight jaw? I interpret these to mean hate, but Mom (or Dad) would not lie to me and especially God would not lie to me. Therefore my feelings must be lying to me." The net result is that the child learns to distrust personal feelings and looks to others to see what he is "supposed" to feel.

An equally serious result is that the child may think, "Mom and Dad aren't listening to me and don't believe me or trust me, so I'm not about to believe or trust what they say. So, I won't listen to them." This leaves the unanswered question "Who do I believe or trust?" The sad, but common, outcome is that they turn to peers who have the same type of problems but little wisdom to get help and solace.

Parents play a vital role in helping children learn about and process their emotions. The importance of this was addressed in an article dealing with juvenile sex offenders. Gail Ryan, co-editor of *Juvenile Sex Offending* (Lexington Books, 1991), said, "These are kids who are growing up without the basic human skills of empathy. In many cases, parents have put too much emphasis on discipline and not enough on children's feelings.   If we don't appreciate children's feelings, they grow up not appreciating other people's [feelings]."[2]

SO WHAT CAN WE DO?

In the case of the teenage boy who says, "I'm hungry," a wise parent will validate his feelings and offer him a snack, maybe some crackers, a glass of milk, a bowl of cereal, or a sandwich. If the budget will not allow any snacking, then a suggested statement might be, "I understand you're hungry, son. *Nevertheless*, we won't be eating again until five o'clock." With this you have not denied the feelings, just the food.

With the young girl who is angry, ask her what happened and then LISTEN! Let her tell her story without interrupting. When she has finished, ask her how she feels about what happened or what she thinks needs to be done. As she expresses her feelings, let her know you understand and that you might have felt the same way if it had been you. Do not try to teach her any principles at this time, or lecture to her, or tell her what to do. If she asks you what she should do, again ask her what she thinks would be the best thing to do or ask her what she thinks her options might be. If she still wants to know what to do, *SUGGEST* a different way to look at what happened or *SUGGEST* something she might do. *DO NOT TELL HER WHAT TO DO!* After she is allowed to express her hate and anger, it will leave. Do not be surprised, if in the next breath, she asks something unrelated like, "What's for dinner?"

I had a client who said she told her daughter she understood how she was feeling and that she probably would have felt the same way. She said her daughter looked at her wide-eyed and said, "You've never told me that before. Thank you."

THE RULES OF VALIDATION

There are four basic rules of validation and they are: *LISTEN, LISTEN, LISTEN,* and *UNDERSTAND.*

Rule 1 - *LISTEN* to what is being said and the events being related. Give your full attention.

Rule 2 - *LISTEN* to the feelings being expressed.

Rule 3 - *LISTEN* to the needs being expressed.

Rule 4 - *UNDERSTAND* by putting yourself in their shoes as best you can.

By following these four rules, your listening becomes genuine hearing and you have set the stage for meaningful and lasting validation.

TO ARGUE OR NOT TO ARGUE; THAT IS THE QUESTION

Validation will often bring surprising responses. Not long ago Marge and Juli (names changed) were carrying on a telephone discussion in which Marge was asking Juli to give some help to Thelma, an ill neighbor. Juli said,

"I will not do anything for her because she is a crabby old lady!"

Often the response to such a statement is, "Well, she really isn't crabby. You just need to be more understanding." To which Juli would probably say, "Oh, yes she is crabby. You don't have to deal with her like I do, so you don't know."

As you can see these are the seeds of an argument. How can it be handled differently?

Marge knew how to validate and instead said, "Yes, she is crabby." Actually, Thelma *was* crabby much of the time and was no fun to deal with. Now see what Juli's actual reply was: "Well, she is probably crabby because of her bad back problems. Maybe I could help her some." When Juli's comment "She's a crabby old lady!" was validated with "Yes, she is crabby," then Juli had no need to defend her position.

The idea of validation is to be able to view

something through the eyes and feelings of another person. When you discount either of these, the seeds of an argument are planted and it may appear you aren't listening or you really don't care. Or, it may seem you are more interested in giving advice than being genuinely helpful. Realize that each person has her own set of feelings and experiences, and that you can attempt to understand them from what she says. Such understanding builds friendship far beyond the need of the particular moment.

GET OUT OF MYSELF FOR A WHILE

When a person validates another person, it does not discount self or change a person's own experiences or feelings. The person listening may be thinking, "If you could only see that situation through my eyes, your problem would be solved," or "Hurry up because I have the answer you need," or "This isn't as important as my problem." Notice how each of those feelings is self-oriented.

Validation means getting out of the "self" orientation and into "other" orientation. By using the four rules of validation, LISTEN, LISTEN, LISTEN, and UNDERSTAND, this can be accomplished. Remember, you don't need to solve the other person's problems. You can listen without guilt. You can try to understand what is going on with the other person without the pressure of coming up with the answer. In the following chapters you will discover how people who are listened to and validated will often come up with the right solutions for themselves.

A client told me he was talking with his best friend, sharing with him some of the things going on in his life and some of the problems he was facing. He said:

> *To practice the principle of validation takes so little time, yet it means so much.*

Part way into the conversation, my friend broke in and said, "You're such a strong person, I know you can handle all of that. Oh, by the way, I wanted to tell you what happened to me." All of the sudden I felt very lonely. I thought he was my friend and he really cared about me, but I guess that's not totally true.

IT TAKES SO LITTLE TIME

To practice the principle of validation really takes little time, yet it means so much. I have often heard the statement, "We have lost some of the old fashioned values. It would be nice to return to a simpler time when the individual had real meaning." I think the simpler time was when we did take time to listen to each other. Stephen R. Covey, in his book, *The 7 Habits of Highly Effective People,* stated the following:

To relate effectively with a wife, a husband, children, friends, or working associates, we must learn to listen. And this requires emotional strength. Listening involves patience, openness, and the desire to understand—highly developed qualities of character. It's so much easier to operate from a low emotional level and to give high-level advice. [3]

I believe there is no better place to experience this than at home with your spouse and children. We can teach each other to trust in self and to believe that personal feelings are valid. We can help each other know that solutions can come from within self and one does not need to always look to someone else. When one learns this at home, it spreads to the next level of the world around us, opening the way to gain knowledge from others and broaden our ability to make more informed personal choices.

BEGIN TODAY

Validation is much easier if each person is in touch with his own feelings. Most people know the feelings are there, but they either deny or stuff them. The result keeps us from being in touch with ourselves. In order to be in touch with your emotions, pause momentarily three or four times today (and each day for the next week) and ask yourself, "What am I feeling right now?   Call to mind the menu of emotions: Mad, Sad, Glad, and Afraid.   Remember, you can be feeling more than one emotion and that may bring about the feeling of frustration.   Break down what you are feeling to one or more of the four emotions listed above.   Then ask yourself this question, "What is causing this emotion?" or "What event is this emotion hooked to?"   Doing this much will help you acknowledge yourself as a real person with needs, wants, and feelings.

If you are willing to go farther, then ask yourself, "What are my choices or alternatives to handle my emotions or problem?"   Now comes the hard part and that is giving yourself permission to let your mind think of a wide range of possibilities. Usually we stop ourselves at only one or two possibilities.   If you will practice looking at a wide range of choices, even some crazy sounding ones, you will generally come up with a good choice that will work for you.   When you are practiced in allowing yourself that freedom, it will help you give others the chance of looking at a wide range of choices for their needs.   Thus you begin to practice walking with yourself and others emotionally.

Chapter Four

---•••---

Principle 4
Develop The Art Of Listening

LISTENING IS AN ART

Interpersonal communication is one of the most difficult challenges we face. This challenge started when we were born. Each of us had to learn how to make our needs known without being able to speak any words, and we soon found out how frustrating this was for us and our parents. I have watched as a baby cries or points at something and an adult tries to interpret what the baby wants. Sometimes the adult guesses correctly, resulting in smiles and coos, and other times the child points again and again with resulting frustration and anguish from both parent and

> *In the art of communications, the primary key is the ability to listen.*

child.

As time passes, the parent works at teaching the child words associated with objects, needs, and feelings. The child attempts to mentally build an association table in its mind and tries to form the words with his mouth. At the same time, the parent tries to form an association table of the word attempts of the child. Thus, the art of communication begins.

The primary key is the ability to listen. It seems like it should be so easy since we are all born with the instrument called ears and the intricate mechanisms inside the ear to process the sounds. Surely, since we all have the same equipment, we ought to be able to hear just alike. Unfortunately, it doesn't work that way. Because of each person's emotional and cultural experiences with words, they sometime mean different things to different people. This process is complicated even more when hearing and sight are impaired. Other communication skills have to be learned, such as signing or reading by braille. Whatever the method of communicating, the basic principles are the same.

> *Indirect messages are not clear communications.*

LISTEN FOR INFORMATION

Listening for information is a difficult task to accomplish. Some words evoke emotional responses and can bring about a defensive attitude. This can happen in any setting such as family, marriage, friendship, and business. The questions that often cross our minds are, "What did I do wrong? Why is this subject being brought up now? What do I have to do now? There must be something wrong or the subject would not be talked about now."

During much of our life, some people have talked to us in indirect ways hoping to get across a need without stating it directly. The need may be something as simple as, "My back sure itches," or "The grass needs to be mowed." Now we must look at the intent of these statements. Are they an observation or are they an indirect way of manipulating someone into volunteering to act on them?

Assuming that someone will understand your need rarely works. "My back sure itches" infers, "If you care about me you will scratch my back." Indirect messages are not clear communication. This approach puts the burden on the listener of needing to be overly vigilant

> I am not responsible to solve the problems of everybody else.

lest some hidden message is missed. It is a refreshing moment when we have a conversation with someone who is direct. It is often such a surprise that it takes time to adjust to the directness and the thought may be that the person we are talking with is being pushy, when, in fact, the person is just being direct. For communication to be clear, it is important to remember this: If you need or want something, ask for it. To avoid sounding pushy, do it kindly and respectfully. For instance, "Honey, would you please scratch my back right here?"

During the communication process, many men wonder, "What am I supposed to fix?" Many wives talk in indirect messages and it is extremely frustrating for the husbands who have to guess. They are thinking: "What is wanted? What is needed? What am I supposed to get out of what I'm hearing?"

RELIEF FOR THE LISTENER

Two of the greatest principles I have learned are: (1) I do not have the power to make anything all better for anybody, and (2) I am not responsible to solve the   problems of everybody else. Too often when someone begins to tell us a problem, the internal thought process immediately begins to make us feel the pressure of being responsible to solve the problem and to make everything all better for that person. Feeling responsible, we try to come up with a solution for each aspect of the problem while it is being related and thus miss some of the information.

If these two principles are understood and believed, the pressure is off and you are able to listen completely. That's when true communication occurs. The next step is to let the other person know you are listening and genuinely care. The following two comic strips, *Rose Is Rose* by Pat Brady, speak volumes.

The next day the following cartoon appeared.

(*Rose Is Rose* reprinted by permission of United Feature Syndicate, Inc)

This concept of listening without giving advice was further illustrated in a personal experience related by Rhea Zakich, creator of *The Ungame* game, who had temporarily lost the use of her vocal cords. She reported the following experience with her young son, Dean:

One day during my enforced silence, Dean came home from school shouting, "I hate my teacher! I'm never going back to school again!"

Before my vocal-cord problems, I would have responded with my own outburst: "Of course you are if I have to drag you there myself." But that afternoon I had to wait to see what would happen next.

In a few moments, my angry son put his head in my lap and poured out his heart. "Oh, Mom," he said. "I had to give a report and I mispronounced a word. The teacher corrected me and all the kids laughed. I was so embarrassed."

I wrapped my arms around him. He was quiet for a few minutes. Then suddenly he sprang out of my arms. "I'm supposed to meet Jimmy in the park. Thanks, Mom."

> *Poor questions are offensive, create a defensive attitude, and shut down understanding.*

My silence had made it possible for Dean to confide in me. He didn't need my advice or criticism. He was hurt. He needed someone to listen.[4]

In this example the son knew his mother could not speak. The mother let her son know she was listening by giving him her full attention and putting her arms around him.

Body language and eye contact always let another person know you are listening. What we do with our eyes and body posture assist in validation. If we do not focus our eyes and attention on the person speaking we can give the impression that we are not genuinely interested in them. Often, all it takes is a slight shift in position and leaning toward the other person indicating they have your full attention. Sometimes this can be accomplished by gently touching a person's hand or arm. All of this is done without saying anything. Thus, appropriate silence can become a great validator. Another way to show you are listening is through the use of well-placed nonthreatening questions.

THE ART OF QUESTIONING

Good questions allow people to communicate on a level of mutual understanding. Poor questions are offensive, create a defensive attitude, and shut down understanding. So how does one learn to ask good questions? First, consider your intent. Are you truly seeking to understand the other person? Are you seeking information you don't know? Are you trying to prove your point by using "I gotcha" questions? Are you trying to give the other person some hidden message with the question? Your intent, which is shown in your eyes, voice inflection, and body posture, will probably reach the person before your words do.

Second, look at the type of question because it will give clues as to your intent. I have a tough time with "Why" questions (e.g., Why did you come home so late?) as they are often indirect ways of saying "Defend yourself." Another example is "Why did you spill your milk?" This question amuses me now, but it didn't when I had children spilling milk. Maybe we can see the ridiculousness of it if your five- year-old looked up at you and answered, "Oh, I spilled it because I wanted to see how the milk would run all over the table." The best proof of the

> *Good questions usually start with the following words: how, what, when, where, do, and is.*

usual negative affect of "why" questions is found in the typical answers such questions generate: "Cuz," "I don't know," or a shrug of the shoulders.

Another type of problem question is the question that contains the answer. "You are feeling mad, aren't you?" "You really don't believe what you are saying, do you?" "You agree with me, don't you?" "That's how we feel, isn't it?" "You like broccoli, don't you?"

When dealing with couples where either the husband or wife does this, the other mate often thinks, "There is no reason to answer because she really doesn't want to know. Her mind is already made up and she doesn't want my opinion. All she wants is for me to say what she wants to hear."

Questions that are the easiest to answer usually start with the following words: *how, what, when, where, do,* and *is.* Using some of the above questions and replacing some of the words with the ones just listed, see how you feel. "What happened that made you so late?" "What caused the milk to be spilled?" "How do you feel?" "Do you agree with me?" "What is your opinion?" "Do you like broccoli?" "What vegetables do you like?" The intent of these questions is to find out information or to understand the other person better.

Earlier in the book, we mentioned the need for people to go emotionally to a level that allows them to process their feelings adequately. There is an art to questioning that allows you, the listener, to follow people to that level without trying to change their direction. Remember, you do not have to change your own values, opinions, or beliefs when walking emotionally with another person and ideally, you won't be trying to change theirs either.

OPERATIVE WORDS

The art of questioning employs the skill of listening without translating what you heard. A listener must hear the exact words used because they are the clues. They are the *operative words* that need to be used in the questions. If you translate their words to your words then they will believe you are not really listening to them. Individuals use words that have a particular meaning in their lives. By using those words—their words—you will not only be perceived to be listening carefully, you will also be perceived as understanding what they are saying.

This, however, is *not* reflective listening nor parroting what the other person says. When reflective listening is used, there is the feeling of being in an echo chamber and it seems crazy. It is like everything I say must be said twice for you to get it. I believe the overuse of this listening technique is demeaning. Whereas, the use of operative words allows you to follow a person's lead without diverting her attention with your repetition of what she just said.

The operative words a person uses lead to the place a person needs to go. If someone says, "I am feeling very sad." The operative word is "sad." So your question could be, "What is causing the sadness?" The answer may be, "My children are having such a hard time." The operative words are "hard time." To that you could ask, "Oh, I'm sorry to hear that. What are they having a hard time over?" Or "What's causing their hard time?" When formulating questions around the operative words, remember to use *how, what, when, where, do,* and *is,* instead of *why.*

When operative words are used, the listener focuses on listening. The person talking can know that he is being listened to because he hears his lead being followed. His path is not being challenged or diverted, and the processing of what is needed flows on.

Each of us has developed a perception window through which we view life and its happenings. This window is made up of our life's experiences and teachings. It is like the lens of a pair of glasses made to the needs of our own eyes. It is rare to have a pair of glasses work exactly the same for any two people. Therefore, it is important to spend the effort of concentration to attempt to look through their perception window by understanding their words and how they are used. If you don't understand a particular word, or how it is being used specifically, gently ask with a question such as "You say (give the word or words). I think I know what you mean, but I'm not sure." Then follow with a question: "Can you help me understand exactly what you mean?"

I have listened to couples as they attempt to communicate with each other. One will state what they are needing, then I will ask the other to tell what they heard. It is amazing how the words are changed and the meaning totally misunderstood. During one session, a husband said, "I would like to know where you are going when you leave." What the wife heard was, "You don't trust me and you want to control me." He explained to me, "All I wanted to know was where she was going in case I needed to get in touch with her for some emergency." This is a simple example of the many times I have heard inaccurate translations of words and thoughts. This example effectively points out not only the need for careful questioning but careful listening to—and understanding of—the response.

The next time anyone starts to tell you what happened to them, listen very closely and follow the operative words. Remember, you don't have to make it all better and you do not have to come up with a plan. Just listen, try to understand, and show that you care.

THE GREAT INVALIDATOR

There is a word we use in the English language that has the power to invalidate even the kindest, most caring comment. See if you can pick it out in the following scenarios.

• Your eight-year old comes home from school and is all excited about a picture he drew. He grins from ear to ear as he shows it to you, pointing out the good grade his teacher gave him. You look at it, smile proudly and say, "That's really a good picture, but you got dirty finger prints all over it."

• Your employee comes to you with the written report you requested. You thumb through it, smile and say, "This looks good, but I see I'll have to cut some things out of it."

• You are talking with a friend about a piece of furniture he needs to move. He says, "It's no problem. I think I'm strong enough to move it myself. You respond with, "You're strong, but not that strong. You'll need some help."

• You and your mother have had a disagreement. You say to her, "I love you, Mom, but we've got a problem we need to resolve."

Obviously the invalidating word is "but." No matter how nice the comment is preceding the word "but" the comment following it is what will be remembered. Henry Ward Beecher said, "The meanest, most contemptible kind of praise is that which first speaks well of a man, and then qualifies it with a 'but.' "[5]

The "but" phrases are mostly negative comments. If you are giving a compliment then I suggest you stop before the "but" statement and leave the rest out. For instance, when the child showed the mother his

> *No matter how nice the comment is preceding the word "but" the comment following it is what will be remembered.*

picture she could concentrate on the picture and just say, "That's really a good picture." Period. Now it is a genuine compliment without the invalidating qualifier. Ignore the fingerprints—they are of no consequence. In the instance of the employee's written report there is no need to say, "but I need to cut some things out of the report," even if you do. That can be mentioned later when you explain what had to be done. It's sad to put a damper on a job well done with a "but" comment.

Sometimes you can include what you want to say without invalidating your first statement. In place of the word "but" you can sometimes use the word "and." In the case of your friend moving a piece of furniture, the "and" substitute works. You could say, "You're strong all right, *and* I would like to give you a helping hand. Would that be okay?" Also, in the situation with your mother you could say, "I love you, Mom, *and* we've got a problem we need to resolve."

I strongly urge clients to get rid of the "buts" in their conversation. They nearly always invalidate whatever validation was given.

THE EYES GIVE CLUES

It has been said that the eye is the window of the soul. I have found this statement to be true. The eyes tell so much about a person and give clues concerning what is going on within that person emotionally. I have observed a number of reactions that are indicated by the eyes. I have checked out my beliefs with different people, after our conversation was completed, and they confirmed my observation. One reaction is the person I am talking with will intently study my face while he tries to decide what *he* thinks *I* think he should be feeling. He is looking outside of himself to see what he should be feeling. Often things are said by someone to test my facial reaction to see if the answer will be acceptable.

Another reaction is that the listener stares off into space and their eyes seem to be glassed over. This reaction is often seen in a teenager. The message the teenagers seem to be giving is, "I am not interested in what you say." In therapy, when I have asked such a teenager what he is feeling he has said, "I don't believe my parents listen to me or believe me, so why should I listen to them?" This usually comes as a result of a lecture or from statements that tell him what he "should" or "ought" to be feeling. A third reaction is the eyes will shift rapidly from place to place showing a feeling or belief that it is not safe to talk freely.

Probably the most significant reaction is this: the eyes will shift slightly down and to one side and defocus. This means they seem to be comfortably resting without the need to focus on any physical object. Usually, this is a momentary shift. During this time the person goes inside to see what he is feeling. This signals that the individual is feeling the environment is safe and you are nonthreatening. In a discussion with friends or children, this is often a good clue that the question asked is clear, nondefensive, and nonthreatening, thus allowing the person to go inside and consider what is being said. Then the eyes will return and look at you as the person answers.

BEGIN TODAY

Observe your listening patterns. Do you listen completely or are you thinking of solutions while the other person is talking? Are you impatiently waiting to give your point of view? Do you automatically jump in when the other person takes a breath or pauses to think through a thought? In the next conversation you have with someone today, listen by giving your full attention. If you start to formulate any answer while they are talking, refocus your mind to listen completely. One of the greatest compliments you can give to another person is your complete attention.

Chapter Five

—•••••—

Principle 5
Find The Right Time To Teach

WHEN DOES LEARNING OCCUR?

Life is not filled with *only* validation. But it is through validation that we set the stage for effective teaching. We have the responsibility to teach children (and at times each other) values, principles, and new information. We want to find the best time and way to do this. So, how and when do we do it?

We have been told that learning occurs at the right teaching moment, and when that moment comes, we must seize it and take advantage of it or it may never come again. The problem is, too few of us know how to recognize the "right teaching moment." Have you tried to teach something in the heat of the moment? How well did it work? Either an argument begins or the person you are trying to teach says, "You just don't understand," and leaves. So when does learning take place?

One kind of learning happens when someone crosses over a boundary that has a consequence. Here are a few examples: a child learns how many times the parents will say "no" before they blow up; a driver learns how far he can exceed the speed limit before he will likely be ticketed; a child plays with fire until he gets too close and gets burned. This kind of learning often happens after the fact and comes from the school of hard knocks, which sometimes has serious consequences. One of the emotions associated with this kind of learning is fear.

Another kind of learning occurs when there is a need or a desire to find out something you don't know or fully understand. When we are with someone who might have that information, and there is an atmosphere of safety, we are ready to be taught. A simple example of this is a child wanting to learn how to make cookies or build a kite. Or, consider the young child who says, "Daddy, where do butterflies come from?" If too busy to answer, Dad may miss a prime opportunity to interest and educate his child about nature. What

> They learned because they trusted their teacher.

caused the child to ask that question at that time? Maybe he just saw a butterfly. Will he be as interested in learning about it later? Maybe not. Taking just a few minutes and briefly explaining the process or referring to the encyclopedia can help the child experience an exciting discovery. When children are responded to, they discover that learning can be fun, and that they are important to you.

Another example of learning is the process of going to school. When we are young we go to school because it is the law. As we begin to gain skills in reading, writing, and mathematics in a safe environment, the desire to get more education is kindled. This brings to mind the movie *Stand and Deliver*. This movie was based on a true story about young high school students from a rough neighborhood. A teacher believed in them, challenged them, and taught them higher mathematics. They learned because they trusted their teacher. In the process of learning the math, they learned to believe in themselves. Imagine the outcome if all teaching were approached from the view of helping all students believe in themselves by creating a safe environment.

The following poem catches the spirit of this need and applies to anyone endeavoring to teach anyone else:

A Teacher Is . . .

Someone who senses the
worth of my soul,
Who sees the potential
within.
Who somehow knows how
to open the way
For me to try harder,
and win.

Someone who sees beyond
the small acts
That cover my real needs
inside,
And uses the power
of calm gentleness
While setting the boundaries
that guide.

Someone who opens the
world to my view,
And causes my mind to
explore
The wonders of life
in ways that inspire
A yearning to walk through
the door.

Someone whose smile
reveals a deep faith
In all that is decent
and true,
Whose caring and love
I cannot resist.
That someone, that teacher
is you.

— Joy Saunders Lundberg

The two following situations illustrate how creating a safe environment for learning also works with adults:

Situation 1:

A woman says to her husband, "I've tried and tried and I can't get my computer to do columns. Would you mind helping me?" You tried to explain it to her before, but she wasn't ready to learn. Now she's ready. At times like this, it is demeaning to insult her with something like, "I tried to teach you that before, but you didn't want to know. If you had listened then you wouldn't be having trouble now." That won't accomplish anything. In fact, that kind of comment, even if true, will turn on the "heat" and, remember, the heat of the moment is not the time to teach. Try using a validating phrase like, "That's got to be frustrating." And then, "Sure, I'll be happy to help." Such an approach can do wonders for your relationship.

Situation 2:

A group of friends are having a discussion and, in the course of the conversation, one says, "That might could happen." Another member of the group, an English teacher, can't resist correcting the person and says, "You should never say 'might could.' That's not proper grammar. Instead say, 'That might happen.'" At that point no one can even remember what "might happen" and the conversation experiences an embarrassing silence. This is not the time for a grammar lesson. If the English-teacher friend feels inclined to help the person learn a concept she will do it privately, in a kind and respectful manner, at a later time, even asking permission. For example, she may say "I enjoyed our conversation and wondered, would you mind if I shared a little grammar tip with you?" or maybe just ignore the grammatical error all together.

A neighbor reported that he will never forget a teaching moment his father seized when as a teenager he corrected one of his father's adult associates. When they got home, his father asked him, "Was that necessary to correct him? I don't care how right you are, next time keep your mouth shut." There are times when it is courteous to let things pass without correction. This allows people to maintain their dignity. Even this father waited until they were home, out of the heat of the moment, to teach his son what to do next time, rather than embarrass his son in front of his associate.

> The heat of the moment is not the time to teach.

The important thing in these cases is to create an atmosphere of safety and a feeling of respect. Then, whatever learning there might be will be effective and the people involved will feel greater self-esteem. Otherwise, it won't do anything but create an atmosphere of hostility.

WHY NOT THE HEAT OF THE MOMENT?

The heat of the moment is that moment right after something has happened or while it is happening. During that time when emotions are running at the highest level, and guilt and shame are being keenly felt, a person is feeling defensive and will most likely want to justify his actions. This is *not* the time when anyone is ready to learn.

Some may say, "But that is the time when everything is fresh and all the details are at hand. If you don't use that time, then the greatest impact will be lost. You have got to seize the moment!" I have heard this many times and have to admit that I used to feel that way myself.

Years ago my fifteen-year-old son asked if he could borrow my wire cutters. I told him he could if he would be sure to put them back. I remember this story well because they were my favorite wire cutters. I have certain tools that I almost cherish and these cutters were among them. I didn't think anymore about his borrowing them, until two weeks later when I was walking in the back yard and found them lying in the grass. I picked them up and saw that the cutting surface was badly rusted, beyond repair. I was one upset father. I stormed into the house, waved the wire cutters in my son's face and angrily shouted, "You left my wire cutters out in the grass and now they're ruined! Look at them. How could you leave them out with the sprinklers running on them every day. You said you'd put them back. How could you do this? These are my favorite cutters." I was livid.

Can you guess what he said? I'll bet every parent can. He looked up at me and responded with the ageless answer, "It wasn't me."

In this kind of situation nearly every child says whatever is needed to save his skin. No good thing comes from reacting in the heat of the moment. I wholeheartedly agree with a statement Stephen R. Covey made; "My experience has been that there are times to teach and times not to teach. When relationships are strained and the air charged with emotion, an attempt to teach is often perceived as a form of judgment and rejection."[6] I needed to calm down first, then talk about how to care for tools, and give him the opportunity to pay for a new pair of cutters.

> *Effective teaching can only happen when you are in control of yourself.*

Another example that amplifies *when* and *when not* to teach happened when our thirteen year-old son was hit by a drunk driver while riding his bicycle. He had been delivering newspapers and had been told to come right home when he was finished. Instead, he decided to visit a nearby convenience store. In order to get there, he had to ride along a dark, heavily traveled street that had no shoulder or sidewalk to ride on. When we arrived at the scene, the paramedics were there and our son was pretty banged up. Yes, he had disobeyed. Yes, he had gone on a dangerous street at rush hour. Yes, we were upset and worried. Yes, his new bike was destroyed. Yes, this wouldn't have happened if he had obeyed. In this incident it is easy to see that this was not the right teaching moment. So, when is?

First and foremost, effective teaching can only happen when you are in control of yourself. If you, as a wife, husband, parent, neighbor, friend, boss, or worker, are angry or out of control there is no way any real teaching or learning will take place. You will likely say things you will regret saying and defensive attitudes and arguments will erupt. It is only after those involved are calm that there can possibly be a teaching moment. In our son's case that didn't happen until he was home from the hospital and feeling better. And the interesting thing about it was that he was the one who did the teaching. "I shouldn't have gone to the store," he said. Instead of zeroing in on more of what he had done wrong (there was no need—he understood), our conversations turned more to talking about the effects of drinking and driving, something he now had strong feelings about. It turned into a good learning experience for everyone in the family.

Another good example of the importance of controlling self in these types of situations was shared by the father of a fifteen-year-old boy.

> I was driving my son home on a winter day when the road was snowpacked and extremely slick. Just after arriving in our neighborhood, in a playful mood my son said. "Let's do donuts," and he pushed his foot on the brake and jerked the steering wheel. He jerked it only a little but we still went out of control. The car skidded harmlessly to a stop but we were both shaken.
>
> I chose not to say anything, assuming he must have fully realized how stupid and dangerous a thing he had done—and how little it takes to put a car out of control on a slick surface. When we got into the garage, I asked him calmly if he had learned anything. He quietly but sincerely said that he had, and I responded that there was nothing more that needed to be said, either between us or with anyone else. He has never forgotten it—for two reasons: he learned from the lesson taught by the car and he still appreciates having been treated in a validating manner.

Sometimes the teaching moment is the experience itself and by belaboring it we diminish its affect. In instances like this, self-respect is preserved.

NOT ALL QUESTIONS NEED IMMEDIATE ANSWERS

The recognition of the teaching moment is more likely to happen if we change the label from "teaching moment" to "learning time." I have heard it said when someone asks you a question, they are ready to learn. This may or may not be true, depending on what you do with it. There are times when I really want to talk through a problem with someone and I don't want them to teach me anything or fix anything. I just want to bounce around ideas to see how they sound. It is a discovery process. When a person is in that discovery process it is the perfect time to use validating phrases and questions. Then it can become a genuine learning experience, not from what someone else is saying, but rather from what is discovered within themselves.

When a person says "What do you think I should do?" the natural tendency is to tell the person what to do. In other words, you try to take the responsibility for their problem. How many times have you done that and heard the reply, "Oh, that won't work" or "I couldn't possibly do that?" When you get that reply you may think, "If you didn't want my help then why did you ask?" Or maybe you told her what she should do and she later came back with, "I did exactly what you said and it didn't work." You may discover that what you told her to do was not what she did. At that point you may even resolve to never tell anyone what to do again. And the resolve may last until the next time you hear, "What do you think I should do?" It is not easy to resist telling people what they "should" do when they ask us. That's when we must remember that in most cases it doesn't work.

Each time I hear someone ask me what to do, I mentally review my basic concept: I can't make anything all better and the problem belongs to that person, not me. With that in mind, the greatest thing I can do is find out what they have already done and what they would like to do. The way to do this is to directly ask the questions, "What have you tried so far?" or "What would you like to do?" or "What are your options?" Then listen completely without mentally formulating an alternate plan. It is amazing how this relaxed approach allows real learning to take place for both the teller and the listener. In the process of their telling the story, what approaches they have tried, and what further options exist, the best or at least a viable solution often comes out. When that happens, the other

> *After something has happened that needs to be talked about, finding the right time to follow up is important.*

person may say, "Thank you so much for solving my problem." Or they may say, "I've got it! Why didn't I think of that before?" Whether or not you get any credit for helping find the solution isn't important. Your main function in their discovery process was to listen and ask nonthreatening questions.

Rather than telling them what to do, it is helpful to give another view of the problem by saying, "Have you thought of it this way?" or "Are there any other options?" It often opens up a whole new idea for consideration. Or after they have thought of everything they can come up with and they still don't seem to have a solution, if you have an idea that might help, you could say, "Here's a suggestion you might consider. I'm not sure it will work, but it might." Then give your suggestion with no "shoulds" or "oughts" attached. This could be a good time to share an experience you or someone you know had that was similar to the problem at hand. It may stimulate their thinking and help them come up with something even better for them (see Chapter Four - *Develop the Art Of Listening* and Chapter Six - *Learn the Effective Validating Phrases and Questions*).

THE TIME TO FOLLOW UP

After something has happened that needs to be talked about, finding the right time to follow up is important. To illustrate, let's say your teenage daughter sassed her mother and you, hearing it from the other room, came in and yelled, "Don't you ever speak to your mother like that again!" Then your daughter ran to her room crying. When is the teaching time? Consider the greater impact if you wait until you have both cooled down. Then you can calmly knock on her door and say, "Do you have a few minutes now? I'd like to talk with you." If your voice sounds gentle and respectful she will likely invite you in. If she doesn't, she's not ready, and that's a signal for you to wait until she is. When you do go in for the talk you might approach the conversation with a validating comment like, "It's awful when we have these blowups. I'm sorry I yelled at you like that. Please forgive me. Tell me what happened before I came in." Then just listen and validate without justifying yourself or standing in her way emotionally.

When she's finished, you might reiterate the family value that parents are treated with respect, and suggest that she apologize to her mother. Maybe you can both decide to speak more respectfully to each other and other members of the family. This will do more to teach her respect than any sermon you could deliver on the subject, because she will have seen how you apologized and treated her with respect. I'm not suggesting that you let her sass her mother without interruption. I am suggesting that stopping the sassing respectfully with a follow up later will have a better result.

One father reported how he was tempted to say something at the time an incident happened—in the heat of the moment— but stopped himself and decided to wait until things were calmer. He reported the following:

My son and his wife were visiting in my home when his wife set a glass of water down on the coffee table. My son snapped at her in a demeaning tone, "Don't put the glass there! It could ruin the table. Put it on the paper—that's what it's for." And he abruptly grabbed it off the wood and set it on a newspaper. She was embarrassed. I cringed inside when he said it, even though I knew he was trying to protect our table. He could have accomplished the same thing in a kinder, more caring way. I decided to keep quiet at the time and not make it into a bigger scene.

> *Sometimes, we say too much trying to make the point perfectly clear and we ruin the teaching moment.*

Later when he and I were working on my computer, I told him how I felt about his talking to his wife like that. He needed to know how hurtful it sounded, and that his wife and her feelings were more important than the table. I did not belabor it; I just mentioned it.

This father was wise not to go into over-kill. Sometimes, we say too much trying to make the point perfectly clear and we ruin the teaching moment. A friend of ours has a saying that fits this situation: "Too much good; no good."

What about the time when your grown daughter calls and pours out her troubles to you? Knowing that the best thing you can do for her at the time is to listen and validate her feelings, you may be wondering when the best time is to share ideas or some of your own experiences that you think might be helpful. I suggest you wait until later and then follow up with a phone call of your own. You could say, "I've been thinking about our conversation yesterday and I want to share some ideas with you that may or may not be helpful. Only you will know if they are. I was remembering when I was in your situation I . . ." and you tell her about your experience and what you did or wished you had done at the time. Or you may say, "Have you considered . . ." and you tell her your ideas. By using this language you can share ideas with her without putting pressure on her to use them. This kind of teaching can stimulate her thinking. However, the caution is that it rarely ever works if you do it at the time she's pouring out her problems. That's not the time she's ready to learn because that is the heat of the moment.

One couple, while proofreading this manuscript, came to the above concept, and it brought to mind an experience they had had. It happened many years ago and the wife had never shared her feelings about the experience with her husband. He reported the following:

> My wife was president of an organization. She had a frustrating experience and was feeling upset; she wanted to give up. She called me at work to vent her frustrations. She was so upset, all I could do was listen to her. The conversation was rather one-sided with her talking and me listening.
>
> Later that day, I knew she would still be upset so I called to follow up with some thoughts I had about her as a person. She wasn't home, so I left a lengthy message on the answering machine. Without knowing it, I must have been validating her feelings and reinforcing her self-worth and importance. She listened to the tape many times over and for several weeks after.
>
> It wasn't until we were reading this manuscript that I knew the impact my message had had on her. She told me, "When I called you, you didn't try to offer advice, you just listened. I needed that. Then later you called and said

> *Teaching a child takes planning and timing. It is important to create an atmosphere that lends to learning.*

just what I needed to hear in that long message on the recorder. By the time I heard the message, I had cooled off and was ready to hear the things you had to say. It made a difference."

PLANNED TEACHING TIMES

Teaching a child takes planning and timing. It is important to create an atmosphere that lends to learning. If there is hostility or contention you might as well forget it because the only thing that takes place during those times is defending and arguing. There are certain situations where a warm and friendly atmosphere can be nurtured and the stage set for genuine communication and learning. Here are a few of those times:

(1) MEALTIME: Sitting around the table with the family is an ideal time for exchanging ideas and views. This kind of family talk is as important to your family's emotional survival as the food being eaten is to your physical survival. Too many families nowadays don't make the time for this important tradition. Popping something into the microwave and eating alone or on the run has become the habit of far too many families. I cannot say enough about how important it is for a family to sit down together for a meal at least once a day. If you can't do it in the evening because of schedules, try breakfast together.

If everyone can't be there, do it with whoever is. If someone is continually missing because of activities and work, then find the time to sit with that child at their own meal at least some time during the week. Mealtimes can be a marvelous teaching time if parents and children are allowed to freely express opinions on a variety of issues, *without criticism*.

One mother uses the indirect approach during this time. She said, "I discuss a news article on a subject I am concerned about. My husband and I talk about it while our children absorb the information. Then they never think I'm preaching."[7]   The discussion needs to be genuine, not contrived or phony. If they sense it is sincere, children will listen. If they have a thought to interject, validate their feelings by allowing them to have and express their own opinion, even if it differs from yours. Expressing it will help them formulate and internalize the family values.

My own experience has taught me that mealtime is not a time to harp on any bad manners or conflicts. That will close the communication window almost immediately. You can talk about these things, another time, after the heat of the moment. To teach table manners you may want to set up a mock formal dinner and talk about them then with everyone contributing even by assignment. It could be fun as well as informative.

(2) BEDTIME: Young children seem especially open to learning at this time. They will do almost anything to delay going to sleep. When our children were young my wife used to lay by them in their beds and tell stories with moral values. They were like little sponges as they lay there in the dark, listening and asking questions. She would often sing with them, too—songs that had messages she wanted them to hear, gentle songs to calm them, or just fun songs that made them feel good. One time she said to me, "The kids don't notice that I don't have a great voice. They just seem to love it anyway."

One of our relatives said, "My husband taught our children many principles through his made-up stories. He had two fictitious characters that had numerous adventures and the children were spellbound. Even now that they are grown he is telling these stories to our grandchildren. If our own children are nearby they always stop what they're doing and listen." She said, "One of our granddaughters said to me one day, 'Grandma, tell me a story—one of those made-up kind.' I told her I wasn't as good at it as Grandpa, and she said, 'That's okay, just start and a story will come.' She was right. I started, a story unfolded, and she loved it."

There are many good books with stories that teach moral principles and ways to deal with life's problems. I recommend William J. Bennett's *The Book of Virtues* as one good source. Another source could be stories from the *Bible*. Reading stories directly from a book will not only teach a message, but may create a love for reading within the child that could last a lifetime. For variety you may want to listen to and discuss an audio tape at bedtime. One excellent resource is a set of audio tapes with music and stories titled *Alexander's Amazing Adventures* by Marvin Payne, Steven Kapp Perry, and Roger and Melanie Hoffman. Accompanying these value stories is an instructional tape for parents by Linda and Richard Eyre, authors of a #1 best selling book *Teaching Children Values*.

Bedtime is a good time for children to open up and talk. And it works with teenagers, too, particularly if it is dark. The darkness seems to give a sense of security because you are not looking at each other's faces. It is a nonthreatening environment. One woman reported the following:

I used to kneel beside the children as they said their prayers. After they jumped into bed I remained on my knees beside their beds and just visited with them when the lights were out. It was a sweet time of sharing a closeness. Even at times when they were in high school they would say on their way to bed, "Come up and talk to me, Mom." I loved it!

You may also try sitting on the edge of the bed when your son or daughter is in bed and talk—without chastising, or moralizing—just sharing an experience or story that was meaningful to you. Even if they groan, validate their feelings and go on, saying something like, "I know you're tired and I won't take long. I just wanted to share something with you." Keep in mind that brief is usually better than lengthy. The best thing that will come out of this kind of sharing is that the child will know you love her. There's an old saying that always rings true: *I don't care how much you know until I know how much you care.* Feeling your love will open their minds to hearing what you have to say. If they start to talk, listen. When they share their own feelings and experiences with you, you will be able to better understand them and the needs they have.

> *Keep in mind that brief is usually better than lengthy.*

Talking in the dark works well with couples too. It allows your mate to share feelings and experiences she or he otherwise may not share.

(3) FAMILY TIME TOGETHER: Some families set an evening each week that is dedicated to uninterrupted family time together. Parents guard this time, making no other appointments, and children agree to do the same. At different times they play board games, share interesting things they've learned

that week, have different family members prepare short lessons with a message relative to the family's particular needs or interests, go skating, bowling, to the circus, a concert, or some other event they will all enjoy. As you are involved in these events together, many opportunities for teaching and learning spontaneously occur. Having a good mix of activities works well and keeps it enjoyable. This is also a good setting for discussing and making family rules, allowing the children to be part of the process. Special treats to eat always make these evenings more enticing and fun for everyone. Good food works wonders in opening up the mind.

One little eight-year-old girl told about a family time her family has at the beginning of every school year. She said, "Dad reminds us that we should always do our own school work. He says it's better to be honest than to cheat for a higher grade." That traditional family time together gives her parents the opportunity to teach their children their family values. And it seems to be working. The little girl told how a friend, who sat next to her, leaned over at the beginning of a test and asked her if she would help her with the answers. She remembered what her dad had taught her, she said, "I knew if I helped my friend cheat, I would be cheating too. So I shook my head no. The next day, the teacher called my friend and me out into the hall and said our answers were the same. It was easy for me to look at the teacher and tell her I didn't cheat. When I looked at my friend, she was crying. She told the teacher she had looked at my paper. I was really sorry for my friend, but I was very glad I had been honest."[8]

Single parents can accomplish wonders by creating this kind of time with a child. One divorced man, who was not the custodial parent, was spending the day and evening with his young teenage son. They had been playing golf, eating dinner out, and were returning to the boy's home. When they arrived it was dark. He said, "My son began to ask some questions about life. It was the perfect time to teach. When it's dark and we're alone seems to be his favorite time to ask the deep philosophical questions, and we discussed some serious issues that night. Just before he got out of the car he leaned over, gave me a hug and said, 'Thanks, Dad. I love you.' "

(4) WORKING TOGETHER: Working side by side provides great opportunities to teach a child. It is amazing how a child will open up during this time if there is a feeling of comradery. Though children need to learn to do some household or outdoor chores by themselves, we can find it very rewarding to continue to work with them on some of those tasks. Obviously, it's the best way to teach them how to do the task properly.

However, we all know that teaching will not be effective during this time if there are feelings of hostility between parent and child. We can keep those feelings at a minimum by using our validation skills during this time as the child makes mistakes and tries again. As we work along together, opportunities to talk about what's happening in their lives and how they can prepare for their future will naturally evolve.

(5) LEARNING EXCURSIONS: This type of teaching has been effectively used in schools for years under the name of "Field Trips." Occasionally, taking a child or the family to a place or event with a specific purpose in mind can help. Years ago we took our three pre-teen and teenage children to a meeting where a cancer surgeon was speaking on the effects of tobacco on the body. We had heard his presentation was graphically poignant and effective. We thought this experience might be the clincher in helping our children decide not to use tobacco. It was one of the most explicit and moving presentations I've seen on the subject. Recently, our grown daughter, who was twelve years old back then, said, "I never forgot what that doctor said and the terrible pictures he showed. That did it for me. I've never used tobacco in any form and never will."

One mother, whose son had talent but was struggling with his desire to practice his piano lessons, took him to piano concerts as often as she could. The exposure affected him and he learned to love playing the piano. Now, as an adult, he earns a good living as a composer and pianist. Other parents with a son prone to stealing made arrangements with the nearest prison and took their son there to see firsthand the results of stealing. It had a powerful effect on the boy.

Many families have a regular weekly excursion by taking their family to church. That's another place where someone else can help you with your teaching responsibility. It can also stimulate conversations on the way home where you can discuss the subject of a sermon or a class lesson and how it applies to your family.

The many kinds of excursions are limitless. All you need to do is examine your child's needs and then boldly seek opportunities to take him or her to places that will teach without you saying a word. It will take some time, but in the end it may be a significant influence for good in your child's life.

(6) NOTES AND TELEPHONE CALLS: Notes or brief letters and telephone calls can provide teaching and learning moments. One friend tells of a minister in Washington, D.C. who used both notes and calls to express love, concern, and counsel to members of both his congregation and members of his family. Being in a demanding military assignment required that he leave for work early and come home late, often six days per week. He took advantage of spare minutes at work to call individuals on the phone, even if only to say "I just called to say I love you." His

children have fondly reported being pulled from class
at school for an "emergency,"
only to find it was their dad
calling from the Pentagon to say
how proud he was of them. On
Sundays, he was often seen
pulling a card from his pocket
and writing a note. He would
deliver some notes personally

> *One of the most important things we can do is to teach our family that we love them.*

immediately after services or the notes would appear
in the mail. He was a master at creating time for those
he cared about whether he was physically available or
not. Everybody loved him—and listened to him.

A telephone call to a spouse to talk over a
problem, apologize, or to express concern, an idea, or
just an expression of love can be extremely valuable if
work and other causes require separation before
something that needs to be said can be said. One of
the most important things we can do is to teach our
family that we love them. It makes all other teaching
acceptable.

MAKE IT HAPPEN

This chapter barely touches on the many ways
and times to teach effectively. The purpose here is to
stimulate your thinking and help you discover times
when teaching your children and others can be most
effective. Teaching is vital if we want our children,

our spouses, our employees, others, and ourselves to learn. We just have to remember that there is a right and a wrong time. If we want learning to take place, we must be willing to keep our cool and find the right time to give the right message. Those who use a little humor and have some fun as they teach will find a much more willing learner. Sometimes we just need to *lighten up*.

Some of the greatest teaching times of all come every minute of our lives as others watch us striving to live the principles we are trying to teach. It is true, we can't be perfect in all things, but we can be continually trying to improve. This effort will deliver a sermon far more effective than words ever can. It has been wisely said, "How can I hear what you are saying when what you are doing is thundering in my ears."

Teaching does not make anything all better for anyone. It does, however, expand people's knowledge and view of new alternatives and possibilities, allowing them to have a broader picture of what can be done in life. This gives them the opportunity to come up with the best solution for their own needs.

In all our teaching, if we remember to apply the four basic rules of validation—*listen, listen, listen* and *understand*—we will be able to create a happy environment for learning. With a little extra effort we *can* make it happen.

BEGIN TODAY

Look at your own situation in life and decide who it is you have a responsibility to teach. Examine the pattern you have used in the past and decide how you can change or improve it. Begin by choosing one of the six planned teaching times discussed in this chapter. Decide what you want to teach. Remember that listening and validating is a vital part of teaching. If you are married you may want to discuss your teaching plan with your spouse. Unity between parents creates the most effective teaching possible.

Chapter Six

Principle 6
Learn The Effective Validating Phrases And Questions

VALIDATING PHRASES

The more you practice validating, the more rapidly the appropriate validating phrase will come to your mind during conversation. Soon it will become automatic. A word of caution: many phrases can have their meaning changed by our tone of voice. Take, for instance, the simple word "Oh." Depending on the voice inflection it can be challenging, sarcastic, condescending, discounting, ridiculing, surprising, questioning, or show that we are sincerely listening. It all comes back to our intentions. In order to be validating, our responses, short or longer, must be *kind, gentle,* and *respectful* with the intent of understanding the other person. *How* we say them has everything to do with how they are received.

Some of you who are new at validating may wonder if these phrases work well when the people you talk with already know the phrases. The answer is yes. They always work when your intention is to truly care about and understand the person you are talking to. It won't matter at all if they know and even use the phrases themselves, because it feels so good when someone sincerely cares.

Here are some effective phrases that seem to work well. Others will come to you as you apply the validating principles.

- Oh.
- I'll bet that's hard.
- That would hurt.
- I think I understand.
- Hmmm.
- I think I might have felt the same way.
- That must be frustrating.
- I'm so sorry that happened to you.
- Wow!
- That's interesting.
- What a difficult position to be in.
- That's awful!
- I don't blame you one bit.
- That's wonderful.
- That was good.
- I'm happy along with you.
- I'm happy for you.
- I'm sad with you.

- That's painful.
- I'll bet that was difficult.
- I feel like crying, too.
- What an awkward situation to be in.
- That was amazing.
- I'll bet that was fun.
- That's neat.
- I'll bet you'll miss him.
- I would have been embarrassed, too.
- That's exciting.
- I never thought of that.
- What a good idea.
- What a good way to handle that situation.
- That just might be the best solution.
- Well, if that doesn't beat all.
- Oh, my goodness.
- Oh, no! I know how much that meant to you.
- That's a tough spot to be in.
- That's a real bummer.
- That's great!
- Tell me more.
- That's got to be a real challenge.

VALIDATING QUESTIONS

Asking the right question is vitally important in helping someone go inside themselves to discover the solutions to their own problems. Without these questions they will fall back on their own question of "What should I do?" Remember, you don't have to solve their problem. In fact, you don't even have the power to solve it. However, you can help them by

> *Keep in mind that your intention is to show that you genuinely care about them; therefore, your questions will be asked in a kind, gentle, and respectful manner.*

asking the kind of validating questions that will lead to the exploration of their own feelings and desires, and to their own best solutions.

Keep uppermost in mind that your intention is to show that you genuinely care about them; therefore, your questions will be asked in a *kind, gentle* and *respectful* manner.

Here are a few effective questions to get you started.

- Oh?
- How did you feel about that?
- What did you do?
- And then what did you do?
- What would you like to do?
- When do you think it could be done?
- What do you think the outcome will be?
- What do you think might work?
- What do you think would work next time?
- Are there other options?

- What happened?
- How did it happen?
- Where did it happen?
- When did it happen?
- What did you think when it happened?
- How could you stand that?
- How did you stand that?
- And then what did you say?
- What do you think caused the problem?
- What's wrong?
- What went wrong?
- What was that like?
- Did you enjoy that?
- Did that hurt your feelings?
- What does that mean?
- What would you like me to do?
- Is there anything I can do to help you?
- Would it help if I (name something you can do)?

As mentioned in chapter four, *Develop the Art of Listening*, there are some questions that immediately bring a defensive answer and many of them start with the word "why." For example: Why did you do that? Why were you late? You'll accomplish far more if you use one of the more caring questions such as, "What happened?" The "why" questions just don't have any good answers. They are mostly used in anger or disgust. Questions that back people into a corner don't help. If you get out of the habit of using them and into the habit of using gentle more validating questions, your children, spouse and everyone you care about will be more likely to open up to you. Then good solutions can be discovered and applied.

The key to validating phrases and questions is that they do not supply any answers in them. They parallel the feelings and expressions of the person you are listening to and do not put your interpretation on what you are hearing. If you supply an answer within the phrase or question, you cease to validate because all you want is to have the other person confirm what you are thinking. An example of supplying an answer within a question is, "Don't you think you ought to do. . . ?"

Validating questions are designed to learn more about the person or the situation. When you ask, "What do you think can be done?" you leave the responsibility where it belongs, and encourage the person to go inside and come up with a personal solution that will work for him or her.

BEGIN TODAY

Think of some situations during the past week where you were in conversation with someone in your family, with a friend, or a fellow worker. Think back and try to recall the kind of questions you used. Did they begin with "Why?" If so, rethink those questions and word them in a nonthreatening, more understanding way by beginning them with *how, what, when, where, do,* and *is.* Refer to the suggestions above to help you rephrase your questions.

Use this knowledge and newly acquired skill in conversation with someone today. Watch their eyes and see if they shift and defocus, then return to you as they answer. If they do, then you will know you have asked the right kind of question.

The art of questioning is worth all the effort and practice it may take. It is the way people will know you care about them and you trust their judgment.

Section Two

***

This section contains a wide variety of
examples that illustrate the practical
application of the principles explained in
Section One.

***

Chapter Seven

How Validation Works With Young Children

BEGIN WITH YOUR BABY

It is never too early to start validating your child. Even though a baby can't verbally tell you what she is feeling, she can definitely communicate her needs. Parents learn early to tell the difference in a baby's cries.

> *Wise parents will validate as they try to meet their baby's needs.*

Wise parents will listen to those differences and try to understand the baby's needs. Then they will validate as they try to meet those needs.

Recently I watched our daughter-in-law do this with our two-month-old grandson when he started to cry while lying on his blanket on the floor. She knew he wasn't hungry (since he had recently nursed), his diaper was dry, and she knew it wasn't his I've-got-a-tummy-ache cry. As she picked him up she said, "What's the matter, little guy? Are you bored?" Of course, he couldn't answer, but he could hear her soothing voice validating him, trying to understand his need. She cuddled him a few minutes, then put him in his infant seat on the table where she was working. As she prepared dinner she talked to him about what she was doing, as though he could understand. He was content. His feelings had been understood and validated.

If a baby continues to cry after you have tried every way you know to meet his needs, keep on validating with a soothing voice as you try to distract him, rock him, or put him in his bed. Resorting to anger will get you nowhere and only make the baby, and you, more upset. He may just need to cry for awhile to work out his own problem or if he has symptoms of an illness he may need to see a physician. It won't be long before he will be old enough to tell you what's going on inside, and he will feel safe doing it if he is accustomed to your understanding and validation. It has been wisely said that if you talk to your child when he is young he will talk to you when he is older.

LET THEM FEEL WHAT THEY ARE FEELING

Children face a multitude of problems as they learn and grow. For example, your six-year-old daughter comes whining to you about a boy in her class. "Jimmy was picking on me again. Why can't he just leave me alone?"

What would you do? It has happened many times before and frankly you're sick of her whining about such things. You have told her she needs to ignore him. Another time you told her to stand up to him and "Tell him to leave you alone." Why doesn't she just do what you say? She must not be getting the message, so you think you need to make it perfectly clear this time, and, with a decibel or two added, you proceed with your voice of experience one more time.

Why do we keep doing what doesn't work? As adults we tend to think we have all the answers for our children. Obviously we know more than they do; therefore, it is our divine duty to impart our expertise in large doses to their eager little minds. Sounds good, but it gets us about as far as climbing a snowcapped mountain on waxed skis. We end up right back where we started—or worse. Usually worse, because lecturing, preaching and giving advice doesn't work. In fact they often backfire. Validation does work.

Let's review the whining daughter scene and show how validation works in this case. Your daughter has just unloaded her problem on you. Remember the universal need of every human being is to feel that *I am of worth, my feelings matter, and someone really cares about me.* If you really care about your daughter and how she's feeling, will you brush her off with a "How many times do I have to tell you" lecture? Of course not. Her feelings matter. She matters. How about, with a little tenderness in your voice, saying, "Oh, honey, that's got to be hard. I bet you're getting real tired of it." Then remember the four rules of validation: (1) LISTEN by giving your full attention, (2) LISTEN to the feelings, (3) LISTEN to the needs being expressed, and (4) try to UNDERSTAND. It only takes a few minutes.

As you do this you may hear her say something like, "I really am tired of it. I'd like to beat him up!" Now you must resist a lecture on beating people up. That's not the issue here. That's simply what she's feeling, and remember, what she's feeling really matters. You might say, "I don't blame you. I think I might feel that same way if I were you." And isn't that true? If you think about it, you really would feel that way. You're just being honest.

> *Even a young child can come up with a good solution.*

Notice how these words validate her feelings. It is okay for her to feel what she is feeling. No one can change that, so there is no point in trying. To do otherwise will only frustrate her further. As long as you keep listening and validating, allowing her to feel what she is feeling, she will keep talking until her frustrations are all out. That is the only thing that will change how she is feeling.

If she asks you what she can do to stop his tormenting, it is resistance time again. Of course you think you know the answer, but the answer needs to come from inside of her to be effective. How about responding by saying, "Hmmm. I'm not sure. What do you think would work?" Watch how smart she becomes. Even a young child can come up with a good solution.

GIVE THEM A CHANCE TO SOLVE THE PROBLEM

Too often people think a child does not have sufficient knowledge to come up with a good solution. That is shortchanging children. They have a far greater capacity for problem solving than we realize. What they don't have enough of is opportunities to discover and develop that capacity. Over and over I have observed children's ability to solve problems. Watch and listen to small children playing house or other pretending activities and you'll discover the rather impressive negotiating and problem solving skills they already possess.

One of the most influential developmental psychologists of the twentieth century, Jean Piaget, discovered that children learn very early to do their own problem solving. He gave this illustration about an eighteen-month-old child: "For the first time, Lucienne plays with a doll carriage whose handle comes to the height of her face. She rolls it over the carpet by pushing it. When she comes against a wall, she pulls, walking backward. But as this position is not convenient for her, she pauses and without hesitation goes to the other side to push the carriage again. She therefore found the procedure in one attempt, apparently through analogy to other situations but without training, apprenticeship, or chance."[9]

One evening my wife received a call from our daughter-in-law, Rose, expressing her extreme frustration over her inability to potty train her nearly three-year-old daughter, Jade. She said, "I have tried everything for the past six months and nothing works. It costs a fortune to keep two kids in diapers. Jade will not cooperate and screams if we mention the potty. She won't even let me put training pants on her. Do you have any suggestions?"

Since we were in the midst of writing this book, my wife decided to suggest that Rose try out these principles by giving Jade the opportunity to solve the problem—after all, it was her problem, too. My wife said, "You might try calmly talking to Jade privately; explain the problem, and ask *her* for a solution."

The following afternoon Rose called back and said the following:

You would not believe what happened last night. I took your suggestion and said to

Jade, "We have a problem. Colton is still a baby and needs to wear diapers. Diapers cost a lot of money and since you are a big girl it would help save us some money if you didn't have to use diapers any more. What do you think you could do to help us so you wouldn't have to use any more diapers?"

Jade immediately began saying a string of disconnected words, which she sometimes does when she gets excited. One of the words was "potty." I said to her, "Do you mean you could go potty and that would help?" Jade clearly answered, "Yes, I can go potty." I said, "Right now?" Jade answered, "Yes" and ran to the bathroom, sat on the toilet and went potty. I was amazed.

To help cement it in *her* mind and get a little divine help in the matter, I added a new sentence for Jade to say in her bedtime prayer—"Please help me go in the potty every time."

The next morning I asked her if she wanted to go potty and she said, "Yes," went in and did it. I put panties on her and two hours later they were still dry. I asked her again, "Do you want to go potty?" and again she said, "Yes" and went.

I could hardly believe this. I was so happy I felt like shouting! I was so pleased that I rewarded Jade with a sticker on a chart each time she succeeded, which delighted her. (The sticker chart had not worked previously.)

Jade learned the concept of going potty so well that two weeks later when she woke up sick one morning she said, "Mommie, I need to go potty." She was still wearing diapers at night and when Rose started to take off her diaper so she could go, Jade said, "No, Mommie. My *mouth* needs to go potty." She ran into the bathroom and threw up in the toilet.

I am not suggesting this method will potty train all children. They have to be ready. If you try it and the child does not respond, wait awhile and then try it again. Use wording that will be understood by your child when you ask for her help in solving the problem.

The problem-solving ability children have became evident again one afternoon when I went out to pick up our mail. A little five-year-old neighbor girl was walking home dejectedly from the neighborhood pool. I said, "Hi, Jennifer. How are you doing today?" Jennifer said, "Not good. The boys at the pool are making fun of me." Validating her feelings I said, "Oh, that's no fun." Jennifer replied, "It sure isn't and I'm sick of it. They do it all the time." I said, "That's hard, but I've got an idea you could try."

A little disgustedly she said, "What?" And I said, "How about just ignoring them?" Jennifer said, "That's not a good idea. I've tried it already and it doesn't work." Then remembering the importance of giving a child a chance to solve her own problem, I said, "What do you think would work?" Jennifer

> *Advice says you must, and if you don't you'll disappoint the advice giver and then you'll feel guilty and still have the problem.*

thought a minute and then said, "I think I'm going to have my mom talk to their moms. That will work." Then she went happily on her way.

Given the chance to solve a problem a child may come up with a good answer or she might say, "I don't know what to do." You may need to help her do some digging for an idea. You could say, "Can you think of just one thing you could try?" Give her a few minutes to think. If she senses you are not ready to jump in with an answer, she'll use the silent time to think. Encourage her to keep thinking of what might work. Then if she cannot come up with any ideas you may need to give her a suggestion.

Suggestions are not advice. Remember, advice says "you should" or "you ought" or "you need to," whereas suggestions allow the child to make her own decisions. Advice says you must, and if you don't you'll disappoint the person giving the advice and then you'll feel guilty on top of still having the problem. Also, if you follow advice and it doesn't work, whose fault is it, and who are you likely to discount in the future?

Instead, you could say to your child something like "I wonder what would happen if you . . ." Then give your suggestion. Notice the wording, "I wonder . . ." It suggests an idea to consider, but is not advice. Or you may give some other suggestion you think will help by saying, "Here's something you might try. I'm not sure it will work, but it might." Notice the wording again. You put no pressure on her to use your idea, nor do you make any guarantees it will work. Then make your suggestion, *adding that she may even come up with a better idea.*

Do you see how this process builds a child's self-esteem? Do you see how it sets you free from the responsibility of having to solve all of her problems? Do you see how it empowers her to become her own problem solver? Do you see how she'll be more willing to talk over her frustrations and problems with you in the future when they are far more significant? Validating your children's feelings and allowing them to solve problems will go a long way toward helping them become emotionally healthy and responsible adults.

TRY THEIR POINT OF VIEW

Consider the following two situations that happened as two young mothers were being observed by my wife in a grocery store. Both had young children, three or four years old, following along at their side. As the first mother wheeled her cart past the candy display, the child excitedly said, "Candy! Mommie, I want some candy." As the child reached for a bag of M & M's, the mother abruptly pulled his hand away and sternly said, "No. We're not here to buy candy!" The begging, which is so often the next step in these situations, began. "But I want some. Please, Mommie, please." A little louder the mother said, "What's the matter? Can't you hear? I said no!" Then the tears began. The mother was launched and ready for battle. "You eat too much candy," she preached. "Your teeth are going to rot right out of your head." And she pushed the cart on, only to look back and see the screaming child lying on the floor demanding candy. "Stop crying or I'll never bring you to the store again!" It was an ugly scene that happens far too often. My wife was confused as to who needed the disciplining—most likely the mother.

The second mother came down the same aisle, and her child said the same thing, "Candy! Mommie, I want some candy!" The mother stopped, stooped down to the child's

> *Children have one main job in life and it is to get their own needs met at all cost.*

level, and said, "Oh, doesn't that look good." With bright eyes the child replied, "Oh, yes." The mother then said, "Wow! There's a lot of different kinds of candy here. We don't have enough money for candy today, so we can't get any, but if we could, which one would you choose?" The child looked at all the candy, then, pointing to a bag of peanut butter cups, said, "This one's my very favorite." The mother said, "I bet those are good. The next time I buy candy I'm going to remember that." The child was delighted. And off they went.

What a difference a little validation made. Remember, *walk with the person, let them feel what they're feeling.* Listen to the needs and try to understand. That doesn't mean you need to give in to a child's every demand. It just means you acknowledge and understand the feelings being expressed.

HOLD ON TO YOUR BOUNDARIES

I have a belief that *children have one main job in life and it is to get their own needs met at all cost.* It is only when boundaries are set and maintained that children will eventually grow up emotionally and recognize that others have needs, too. The sooner parents learn to validate and kindly, gently, respectfully, and firmly enforce boundaries, the sooner the child will begin to respect the rights of others.

> *For children to mature, they must learn there are boundaries in life.*

Validation does not change the boundaries; it acknowledges that the boundaries may be difficult.

Maybe children would be less destructive in their efforts to get their needs met if they received a little more validation. When a little one reaches for something she is not allowed to play with, how about saying, "Isn't that pretty. Would you like to touch it?" Then let the child carefully touch it, smell it, and experience it in every way her senses can while you secure the object. Satisfy her curiosity. Then explain that it is not to play with. Often that's all she needs.

This action is respectful of the child's feelings, and eliminates or at least diminishes her, and your, frustration. If she persists, calmly explain it is not to play with and distract the child with a toy, take her to a different room, or put the item out of reach. If the child cries, stay calm and firm. Yelling back at a screaming child only makes matters worse and teaches the child how to yell and scream. Giving in to cries and tantrums tells the child you have no boundaries. For children to mature, they must learn that there are boundaries in life. Setting and keeping boundaries when children are young is crucial preparation for the time when they become teenagers. They will know you mean what you say.

Wise parents can help their children understand their boundaries and what is appropriate behavior, as did the parents of a little two-year-old boy who shared the following experience:

> We could not convince our little boy, Jared, to go to the nursery during Sunday School. We took turns staying in there with him, but as soon as we left, he'd begin screaming and wouldn't stop. He wanted to be with us and nobody was going to convince him otherwise.
>
> Keeping him quiet and satisfied for the hour we were in our own class was impossible. Who wants to wrestle a tiger for an hour every Sunday morning? Not us. We would lose our patience and become angry with him. We wondered why we even tried to stay for Sunday School, and, in fact, started staying away from church more and more to avoid the unpleasant experience with Jared.
>
> Then we learned about validation. We decided to try it. The next Sunday morning we talked to Jared before going to Sunday School. "Daddy and I understand that you don't want to go to the nursery, and that's okay," I said, validating his feelings. "Maybe you're not quite ready for the nursery yet. Maybe you need to be a little older. Until then, you can go with Mommie and Daddy to our class for big people, and sit very quietly while the man gives the lesson." He was one happy little boy to hear this good news.

After a few minutes in our class, he began to wiggle and wanted to get down and run. I took him out, but not angrily. We walked to the nursery, I opened the door and we looked in. "See the children playing with the toys. It looks like they're having fun, but I know you don't want to go in, and I understand. You're not ready yet." I shut the door. "We'll go back to my class where you must sit quietly while we listen to the nice man talk to us." And back we went to the adult class.

Jared sat quietly for a few minutes more, then became rowdy again. Once more I took him gently by the hand and walked to the nursery, opened the door and we looked in. "Oh, look at the children in the nursery," I said to him. "They're having their snack. Boy, that sure looks good." Then I shut the door and said, "but you're not ready for the nursery, and that's okay. We'll go back to Mommie and Daddy's class and sit quietly." And back we went.

I did this for three Sundays. On the fourth Sunday when it came time to go into our adult Sunday School class, Jared stopped at the door, took a firm

> *Getting down on their level physically is an important factor in validating a child.*

stance, and yelled "Nursery! I want nursery!"
I said, "Are you sure you're ready?" "Yes!"
was his emphatic reply. We took him to the
nursery, he waved good-bye to us and has
been going without a fuss ever since.

This is a classic example of the power of
validation. Jared's mother understood his need for
more time, and she let him know she understood. At
the same time, she let him know the boundary and
what was expected of him—to sit quietly in the adult
class. When she took him out she did not allow him
to run or play, but instead took the opportunity to
educate him about the nursery, still acknowledging his
desire to be with her. Then took him back to her class
to sit quietly. She was *kind, gentle, respectful,* and
firm, allowing him to see the nursery as the best place
for him.

EYE TO EYE CONTACT

Getting down on their level physically is an
important factor in validating a child. A recently
remarried divorcee with two young children reported
that her new husband, the custodial parent of his
three, was a master at validating children. "Whenever
his or my children speak to him he gets right down to
their eye level and patiently listens. And those kids
adore him."

She told of a time when their children were not

at home, and the doorbell rang. It was a neighbor's child. "Can Andrea come out and play?" the child asked. "My husband got down to that little child's eye level and said, 'I know how much she would like to play with you if she were here, but she's gone to her Grandma's house. She'll be sad she missed you. I'll tell her you came.' It was a tender scene, and, from the look on the child's face, she felt understood and important."

That's what validation is all about.

PUT YOURSELF IN THEIR SHOES

The following incident reported by a grandmother illustrates the value of putting yourself in the child's shoes as you validate her feelings.

My daughter, her husband and their eight-year-old daughter, Stacy, were staying with us for a month or so as they waited to move into their new home. One morning my daughter and her husband needed to run some errands for a few hours and decided to leave Stacy with us since she was still sleeping. When Stacy woke up she looked for her parents, noticed they were not in their room and began to cry. I immediately went to her and tried to comfort her by saying, "It's okay, Stacy. They'll be back later, and I've got some fun things we can do today."

"No!" she said, crying harder than ever. "I want my mother!" She would not be comforted. At that point I decided the best thing I could do would be to stop trying to talk her out of it and just validate her feelings and let her feel what she was feeling. I put my arm around her and said, "It's no fun to be left behind, is it?" Still crying, she said, "No, it's not! And I don't like it. I wanted to go with them." I said, "I do understand. If I were left behind I would be disappointed, too." She cried a little more, all the time expressing her anger, and then as if a switch had been flipped, she stopped crying and said, "So, what shall we do today, Grandma?" She was content from that point on.

Have you ever wrestled with a bored child while waiting to see a doctor, or for any appointment? When the waiting goes on and on it can become more and more difficult. A mother of a four-year-old daughter told of one such frustrating experience. She took some books to entertain the little girl while they waited for their turn, but after a short time the child became fidgety and didn't like sitting and waiting. The mother said, "In the past during such situations, I would become cross and would tell my little girl to sit still and be patient. It never worked and the fidgeting only increased."

Upon learning about validation and trying it the

next time, she reported a significant change. "When my little girl began to wiggle and complain that she didn't like sitting there waiting, I tried validation. Instead of being irritated by her, I put myself in her shoes and said, 'It's not easy sitting here waiting, is it?' My daughter looked up at me with those big blue eyes of hers and said, 'No, Mommie, it isn't easy.' Then she immediately settled down and began looking at her story books."

One mother of a sixth grade daughter had an "Ah ha" experience with this principle. She had attended one of our seminars where validation was taught. At the next seminar she came in early, literally shouting, "It works! It works!" She was so excited she could hardly wait to share what had happened. She reported:

My daughter has been extremely unhappy with school. Nearly every morning she complains about having to go to school, and after she comes home she complains about her teacher, and how she hates school and all the homework. Her complaining always ends with her begging for home school.

She came home yesterday and, even more emphatically than before, said, "I hate school! I'm never going back. And you can't make me. I want home school!"

I always say to her, "You have to go back. We aren't having home school and that's that!" But yesterday your words, "LISTEN, LISTEN, LISTEN, and UNDERSTAND," filled my mind. Instead of my usual response, I sat down with my daughter and gently said, "Oh, what happened?" She became Mount St. Helens and her feelings just poured out. "I hate school. My teacher's awful. She doesn't understand. And she gives us all this homework and I hate it. It's just too much. I hate it!"

I resisted any comments or lectures on the difficult role of teachers or the value of school and homework. I could see these would not answer her needs. The need was to let my daughter express her feelings without criticism, interruption, or solutions.

> *It is important to have genuine understanding of what the child is going through.*

When she finished unloading, I said, "That's hard. I don't blame you for feeling that way." That was all I said, and I did it with a hug. Then she stood up, and said, "Well, I guess I better get my homework done." The next morning she went to school without a complaint. It's a miracle. Validation really works.

This mother caught the vision of how important it is to walk beside the child, putting yourself in her shoes. When you do this, you will begin to have genuine understanding of what the child is going through.

RESIST RESOLVING

In a study on childhood stress, published in the *Journal of Child Psychology and Psychiatry*, 1988, K. Yamamoto reported that, "While children will cry, scream, and report feeling afraid, sad or happy, my testing indicates they don't necessarily need to have situations immediately resolved so much as to process and express feelings, or be understood by another."[10]

This is clearly illustrated in the following experience told by the mother of a twelve-year-old adopted girl.

We adopted Shari when she was three months old. She was a beautiful baby and seemed to grow even prettier each year. We told her from infancy about her adoption. I always thought that my happiness over adopting her would become her happiness. But that isn't how it works. Every person has their own set of feelings.

As Shari grew she began to show signs of insecurity over her adoption. When it was mentioned, which was not often, she would say, "Don't talk about it." I would say, "It's okay to talk about it, honey. Daddy and I love you. We chose you. You mean everything in the world to us." I kept pumping her full of the positives I knew and felt, trying to change her attitude about it.

When she was ten years old, some of her friends whose parents were our friends and knew about the adoption said, "If you're adopted, then your mother is not your real mother." That day she came running home from school crying her little heart out. It took awhile before she would tell me what happened. I held her in my arms and assured her that, though I wasn't her birth mother, I was her real mother. She calmed down, but her frustrations were still buried deep inside.

Finally, when she was twelve years old, I realized what she needed. No explanations. No reassuring phrases. No more of me trying to solve her problem or change her feelings about being adopted. All she needed was understanding. One day as she was crying I sat down beside her and said, "Shari, I think if I were a twelve-year-old girl like you and was adopted I would feel upset, too. I would wonder why my birth mother gave me away. I would wonder what she looked like, and what kind of a person she was."

She looked up at me with tear-filled eyes and said, "Would you really?" I said, "Yes, I would." "Oh, Mother," she said, "That's exactly how I feel." Then I listened as she shared those feelings and asked questions that had been haunting her. I answered her questions and told her I understood, and that it was okay to feel what she was feeling. Her whole body seemed to relax.

Oh, how I wanted to make it all better for her, but I realized I could not. She would have to come to grips with her adoption in her own way. But I could help her by listening and trying to understand from her perspective. That's the first time I realized what it would be like from the adopted child's point of view.

> *A good dose of validation, along with tender loving care, is what is needed most and will serve the child and you best.*

This mother finally understood that her daughter's feelings had to be validated in order for her to accept and understand her adoption.

WHEN ILLNESS STRIKES

We have all experienced the stress of an ill child. It seems at times that nothing can placate the child. Becoming angry and impatient only makes the situation worse. A good dose of validation, along with tender loving care, is what is needed most and will serve the child and you best. A little bit of, "Oh, I'm so sorry your tummy hurts. That's no fun. Would you like me to sit by you and read you a story?" will do wonders.

Often a sick child will resist taking the very medicine that will make him well. When that happens try validating his feelings with a comment like, "I understand you don't want to take this medicine, even though it will help your tummy ache go away. That's okay to feel that way. Sometimes I think medicine is pretty icky myself. Let's try it again in a minute when you're ready." Wait a few minutes then try again. This may not always work, but you may be surprised how often it will. If it doesn't, then it is time for a gentle and firm boundary, "I understand. Nevertheless, open your mouth and take the medicine now." When we respect children and their desires, it is rewarding to see how well they will respond.

What about children with chronic illnesses or disabilities? They must be able to express their frustrations and sorrows over what has happened to them in order to deal with it appropriately. If a parent is always trying to cheer them up and make them feel good about life, they may be stopping the very thing the child needs in order to bring about his own positive attitude about life. We think we need to make it all better. The sooner we accept that we can't, the better off everyone is. The best thing we can do for a child, or anyone in this situation, is to validate their feelings. They need to be allowed to go down as far as they need to go, and then, if they are being properly validated, they'll bring themselves back up.

One mother of a twelve-year-old boy born with spina bifida, paralyzing him from the waist down, told of her experience with validation.

My son, Michael, has had one surgery after another since he was born. I learned early on that there was no way I could actually know what he was going through, only that it was extremely difficult. All I could do was listen to him and try to understand. Recently he had surgery again, this time to release the hamstring behind his knees so he could straighten his legs and stand in his braces. He had a good attitude about the surgery, knowing the outcome would improve his condition.

Just two days before he would have been able to start standing, he turned in the car and heard a pop in his leg. Though he could feel nothing he was sure he had broken his leg. When he told me, I said, "Maybe it was your braces popping." He was sure it was his leg, and when I saw the swelling I was convinced he was right. The doctor confirmed it.

The leg was put in a brace that went clear to his waist. It was very uncomfortable. On the way home from the hospital he started to cry and said, "This is just one more thing. It's not fair this happened to me." Instead of saying, "Don't worry, son. It'll be all healed up in two months and everything's going to be okay," I decided to validate him and let him feel what he was feeling, and said, "You're right, Michael. It isn't fair. And I'm so sad it happened." He went on to say more about how sad he was. Then I said, "So, what do we do now?" He said, "I'll be okay. I guess there's not much I can do except wait it out. These things just happen in life."

The brace made his leg stick straight out in front of him, and he was too embarrassed to want to be seen by anyone. He said, "But I'm not going to school until my leg is all better and this ugly brace is off." Instead of telling him he had to go, I decided to put myself in his shoes and said, "That's okay. I wouldn't want to go either. You let me know when you're ready to go back." He was relieved. In just a few days he said, "Mom, I need to go back to school, but I'm afraid to. Would you go with me?" I told him I would. I was only there for a couple of hours before he said, "It's okay, Mom. You can go now. I'll be fine." I told him how proud of him I was, and left.

This mother wisely allowed her son to feel to the depth he needed to feel without standing in his way. She couldn't make him accept his problem, she couldn't make him feel good about it, and she couldn't make it all better. All of that had to happen inside of

> *Sometimes people are afraid that a disabled person won't be able to pull themselves up unless the are continually fed PMA's.*

him and because of her validation, he was able to come to grips with it much sooner and face it in his own way, in his own time.

Sometimes people are afraid that a disabled person won't be able to pull themselves up unless they are continually fed PMA's (Positive Mental Attitude). In my experience I only see that attitude stifling their progress, rather than encouraging it. They must be able to express what they are feeling without anyone standing in their way by trying to change their thinking. That only makes matters worse. When they do make progress, that is the time for PMA statements, such as, "Good job!" "I'm proud of you." Or "I knew you could do it."

This was evident to a mother who struggled with her young diabetic son. It was terribly difficult for him to accept the fact that he could not eat desserts and candy like his friends. Even his sisters could eat them, but he couldn't. He too said, "It's not fair! I don't deserve this disease. I want some candy!" His mother allowed him to rant and rave and express all of his frustrations, and agreed with him that it wasn't fair and it must be very difficult. Then she kindly set the boundary by simply saying, "Nevertheless, you may not eat sugar." Of course, she tried to make it as easy as she could by discovering "legal" treats. Still it was difficult. She said, "The only thing that works is to validate his feelings. I can't make it all better no matter what I do." Realizing this lifted a heavy burden from her and made him feel better to not have her preaching to him about it all the time.

THE UNIVERSAL NEED

All children need to know that *they are of worth, their feelings matter, and someone really cares about them*: that is the universal need. Trusting them to deal with their own problems, yet setting boundaries to guide their actions, is one of the best gifts we can give them.

It is our natural instinct to want to heal the pain and distress in the lives of our children. The sooner we realize we cannot make it all better but we can help by listening and allowing them to come to their own understanding and solution, the sooner they can heal themselves and solve the problems they face in their own lives.

BEGIN TODAY

Today when your child comes to you, take that opportunity to listen. Resist telling him what to do. Just listen and validate without trying to change his thinking. Use a validating phrase such as, "Wow, I bet that was hard. What happened?" If he asks for your help remember to allow him to solve his own problem by asking him, "What do you think would work?" If the child is happy about something, enjoy the moment with him by saying something like, "That's great! Tell me all about it."

In either case, if you are tempted to teach your child at that moment, don't. If needed, review chapter five, *Find the Right Time to Teach*, and choose a more appropriate time. For this moment *just listen and validate*. Your child will love it and so will you.

Chapter Eight

How Validation Works With Teenagers

IT'S NEVER TOO LATE

> *Through validation parents have the power to give their teenagers what they might otherwise seek from misguided peers.*

If you did not use validating skills with your children when they were younger, you may think it is too late. Not so. Any parent can begin today and enjoy the satisfying rewards it will bring—almost immediately. Even if your teenager seems to be in that common category of "troubled," your use of validation can cause his or her self-esteem and feeling of being understood to rise dramatically. Too often the thing that leads a teen into inappropriate activities is his need to feel accepted and loved for who he is, as he is. Through validation parents have the power to give them what they might otherwise seek from misguided peers.

As parents we must pay attention to our teens' emotional needs. Remember, the universal need of every human being is to feel that *I am of worth, my feelings matter, and someone really cares about me.* One teenage girl was trying to pour her heart out to her father while he was watching a TV program. In desperation, she shouted, "Dad, would you just stop and listen to me!" She finally got his attention. We must remember that no TV show is more important than a child. If we don't listen when the need is there, they won't likely be in the mood when it is more convenient. If you don't want to miss your TV show, put in a video cassette and record it for later viewing. When they are grown and gone, we can watch all the uninterrupted TV we want. Right now their future may depend upon our giving them the attention they so desperately need.

This was graphically illustrated in an article by a therapist who told of a shaggy-haired fourteen-year-old boy who had been a runaway. He had finally come home, but things were still no better than before. "We give him everything," his mother said. "We don't know what's the matter with him!" The therapist reported that once he had won the boy's confidence, it did not take long to find out what was wrong. "My parents don't care about me. We never do anything together. My father never looks at me when I try to talk to him. My mother's always nagging me about my hair, but she never listens!"[11]

Expressing her appreciation for the principle of validation at one of our seminars, one mother said, "I don't know how many times in the last few months, when my teenage son and I were in a severe argument, he said the words, 'Mom, you just don't listen to me.' I can see I've been doing the wrong thing."

If we want our children to listen to us, we must be willing to listen to them first. A recent public service message on the radio ended with this statement: "It's amazing how much better my ears work when my mouth is shut." Truer words were never spoken, particularly as related to communicating with teenagers.

Our anxiety level seems to increase when a child becomes a teen, and we feel duty bound to preach mighty sermons to them with even greater intensity than when they were younger. What we read and see in the media scares us into this mentality. We need to relax a little, reinforce values in the right way and at the right time, and mostly *listen a lot*. (For information on appropriate teaching times see Chapter Five - *Find The Right Time To Teach*.)

Sometimes their first answer is given to test the waters, to see if it is safe to share feelings.

HELP THEM START TALKING

Some teenagers don't seem to want to communicate with their parents. If they have not been brought up knowing it is safe to express feelings, it can be difficult to open the communication door. The mother of an aggressive, drug-using teenager was asked by a therapist to "stop criticizing and to start making a positive comment whenever she was in the room with her son. It could be a compliment on the color of his shirt or praise for completing a simple task, but her comment had to be pleasant. Within a few weeks, the son began to communicate with his mother and even confided in her about some of his problems."[12]   Once communication begins and validation is used, problems can then begin to be resolved by the child.

When talking to our teenagers we often begin by asking them a question. We need to remember that sometimes their first answer is given to test the waters, to see if it is safe to share feelings. When they find that they are not criticized nor lectured to, just validated and listened to, they can proceed with the real answer to your question. As they proceed, we must remember the four rules of validation: (1) LISTEN by giving your full attention (One boy in my office said, "I know my dad isn't interested. He never looks at me when we talk."), (2) LISTEN to the feelings, (3) LISTEN to the needs being expressed, and (4) try to UNDERSTAND.

Also, it is important to realize that teens, and all people, need to be able to talk at their own speed. I had a teenage boy, who had threatened suicide, and his parents in my office. His over-anxious mother could not stop talking. Trying to get the boy to open up she would ask and re-ask and restate in different ways the same question over and over, never leaving time for him to answer. No wonder the boy wouldn't say anything. He never had a chance. Many times parents ask questions with anxiety or anger in their voice. That does not create a safe environment for the answer to come out. Parents need to learn the value of silence while they wait for an answer.

> *Parents need to learn the value of silence while they wait for an answer.*

In this particular therapy session, after allowing the parents to talk and I could see what the communication problem was, I asked the parents to be quiet while I talked with the boy. After asking him a question I was willing to endure the silence until he finally began to answer at his own pace. He didn't want to be there. I understood. No criticism, no trying to convince him it was a good thing for him to be there, just validating. As he realized that I was listening, he began to tell what was really going on inside of him. As he talked and I continued to use appropriate questions and validation, he began to discover what he could do about the problems that caused his thoughts of suicide. The parents began to see how important it was to allow him to talk at his own pace, without criticism or trying to solve his problems for him.

REINFORCE VALUES

Validation does not change family boundaries or values. To the contrary, it strengthens and reinforces them by opening the way for the child to express feelings about them without criticism. It is a vitally important process for a teenager in gaining his own personal value system. To illustrate, here is how it worked for one mother:

My fifteen-year-old son, Robert, came in after school, slammed his books down on the kitchen counter, and slumped onto a chair, looking extremely agitated. I simply said, "Hi, son. What's the matter?"

He began to unload about his best friend. "Jeff is so stupid!"

Refraining from saying, "Hey, that's no way to talk about your best friend," I said, "He is?"

"Yeah, he makes me sick. Do you know what he's doing?"

He was in high gear and I was not about to put the brakes on. "No, what?"

"He is so dumb," he said. "His mom

starts her full-time job and the very next day he brings his girlfriend home with him. He's a jerk!"

I simply responded with, "Hmmm." On the tip of my tongue was a discourse on the moral dangers of bringing a girlfriend home to an empty house. I bit my tongue.

He went on, "Do you have any idea what could be going on over there right now?" He did not want an answer. He was making a statement, so I bit harder, almost drawing blood, and let him continue.

"He is so stupid! He's gonna get himself in big trouble." He went on to give a magnificent sermon, worthy of the highest pulpit, on the hazards of premarital sex, including the horrors of teen pregnancy, abortion, AIDS, and other social diseases and ills.

I could not possibly have preached a more eloquent sermon. And if I had, he would not have heard one word of it. In all actuality, if I had, he likely would have defended his friend's actions.

When Robert finished I simply said, "I think you're right."

What did Robert's mother do first thing when she saw how dejected her son was? Maybe what she *didn't* do was even more important—she didn't blast him with a PMA phrase, such as, "Cheer up, son. Things can't be that bad." Instead, she listened. By allowing her son to express his feelings without interruption, their family values were reinforced in his own mind. There is no doubt that a lecture from her would have stopped the whole process.

According to clinical psychologist Dr. Ray Guarendi, "Kids reflexively shut down in the face of a lecture. Their eyes glaze over, and they don't register any incoming information."[13] So why do so many people do it? Parents and teachers need to stop doing what doesn't work. To make matters worse, parents prone to lecturing, when they see that they are not getting through, often turn to repeating themselves, or harping. Perhaps on remote occasions some point might get through, but it is much more likely that the lecturing and harping will only be remembered by the teenager as just one more of those times when mom or dad didn't listen.

BELIEVE IN THEM

Often teenagers will express ideas and views that appear to be in opposition to family values. Parents usually tense up and start defending or "selling" the family values all over again, thinking they need to make a strong case against their teen's opposing viewpoint. Don't do it. You don't have to agree with their thinking—just listen and try to understand where they're coming from.

> The more we preach, the more they will feel compelled to keep defending that point of view through their actions.

In the process of speaking their minds, our youth often see the folly of their own thinking. Even if they don't express their realization, they are likely to act upon it. If we interrupt them with our "seasoned" point of view, they must switch into a defense mode, which only strengthens their views, however far from accurate they may be. The more we preach, the more they will feel compelled to keep defending that point of view through their actions. Validation shows we believe in them and their common sense.

My wife confessed how she handled a situation with our son inappropriately, even though she understood the principle of validation. Because our own emotions get so involved in encounters with our teenagers we sometimes forget to validate. It does take practice. Here is her story:

Paul needed a part-time job and had searched for weeks. It's not easy for a teenager to find a job in this college town. Finally, his searching and my prayers were answered when he was hired by a pizza parlor to deliver pizza. The incident I'm sharing occurred after a few months on the job.

It was Paul's day off and he was excited to finally have a whole Saturday to play. He had an all-day date with his girlfriend. That morning he ran out the door saying, "I'll be at Amy's house, Mom. G'bye." He not only enjoyed being with Amy, he enjoyed her family. About an hour after he left the phone rang. It was his boss.

"Is Paul there?"

"No."

"We're desperate. Two people called in sick. I need Paul to come in today. Do you know where he is?"

"Yes."

"Would you please tell him to call me as soon as possible. We're desperate."

"Sure. I'll have him give you a call."

So I called Paul and explained the situation to him, telling him I told the boss he would call him.

In his get-out-of-my-life voice he replied, "I hate it when you speak for me. You should never have told him I'd call him . . . because I'm not going to! This is my day off."

I switched into the mother mode and the speech began. "I can't believe you won't call him. And anyway, you know how long it took to get this job, and how many prayers it took. You shouldn't do anything to jeopardize it. How can you not call him? He's been good to you. For crying out loud, you owe him."

He emphatically said, "I'm not calling him!"

And I said, "Fine! Make a liar out of your mother! Goodbye." And I hung up.

Then I felt terrible. I knew about validation, so why hadn't I used it? I just got too caught up in the emotion of the moment. I thought about his day off and realized that if it were my day off I wouldn't want to go to work either. I just needed to validate that feeling. So I thought, okay, I'll do it over.

I got Paul on the phone again and said, "Paul, this is Mom."

With venom dripping he said, "Yeah, whadda you want?"

At that rude response, all my emotions returned and I said, "I just called to tell you. . . you're a royal poophead!"

Silence. Then I got hold of myself and playfully said, "Just kidding." Then more seriously, "Paul, I called back to apologize. I'm sorry, son. The call from your boss must be tough. I really do understand. I think if it were my day off I wouldn't want to go to work either. I'm just passing the message from your boss on to you."

He softened immediately and said, "Thanks, Mom." Paused a few seconds then said, "I think I'll give him a call." Ten minutes later he was home putting on his pizza outfit, and off he went to work.

Notice at the end how she acknowledged his feelings by saying, "The call from your boss must be tough." And then notice the validation; "I really do understand. I think if it were my day off I wouldn't want to go to work either." Validation is bottom line, deep down, open, honest understanding and empathy at its best.

It is important to note here that this type of validation is not manipulation. Through the years Paul had been taught responsibility and he did not need a sermon on it right now. What he needed was a chance to consider his options on his own. This was not the time to teach. It was the time to validate and understand, even if his choice was not what she would choose. Sometimes we push so hard to get our children to behave the way we think they ought to that we drive a giant wedge between them and us, often pushing them in the opposite direction.

DISCIPLINE WITH VALIDATION

You may be thinking, ". . . but what about our family boundaries and rules?" There is no question they are vitally important and can be enforced right along with the use of validation. Remember, effective boundaries are set by being *kind, gentle, respectful,* and *firm.*

For instance, nearly every parent experiences the frustration of waiting for a teenage son or daughter to come home when it is long past the hour he or she was supposed to be there. Some parents have a set curfew, others work with the teen and decide on a time based on the activity. Regardless, when the time comes and they are not home, we begin to worry that they are in some kind of trouble. Of course we worry. We set a curfew because we know accidents or inappropriate activities are likely to happen after that hour. When the teenager finally comes in, we are so worked up over all the things we have imagined that we fail to validate the child.

Ideally, we would like our child to validate us with a courteous caring comment such as, "Oh, Dad, you must be tired and worried. I'm so sorry to keep you waiting." Give it up. It won't happen. At least not until they learn how to do it by experiencing our validating them.

So how does a parent validate in this situation? Not with an angry "Where were you? You're grounded!" That doesn't work, nor does it build a healthy relationship. Keep your cool and remember that true validation is kind and caring. How about saying, in a gentle way, "I've been worried about you, son. What happened?" Then give him time to respond, and LISTEN. You care about this child and you want him to know it. That doesn't mean you do away with your family values or rules to appease him. No. That would be the opposite of caring.

Suppose he says, "After the game we decided to go to Joel's house and watch a video. I just didn't realize it was getting so late." You could validate by saying, "I understand you were having a good time with your friends, nevertheless, the rule is you are to be home by the agreed upon time. Do you understand?" He will likely answer, "Yes." And maybe even surprise you with "I'm sorry Dad." Continue by saying, "I'm glad you're home safe. Goodnight, son." A good rule of thumb is: nothing good comes in the heat of the moment.

The next time he goes out, make sure you both understand what time he will be home. If he is late again you may want to try what I did with my own son. When he didn't come home well beyond the designated hour, I decided to go get him. I didn't know where his date lived. My mistake. Even though it was late, I called one of his friends who gave me the approximate location. I drove to the area, praying I would find him, and there they were—sitting in the car. I knocked on the window and gently, but firmly, said, "Come home now, son." He quickly took the girl to the door and followed me home.

When we were inside he said, "How could you do that? I'm so embarrassed." I calmly validated and reaffirmed the rule by saying, "I understand that's embarrassing. I hope I don't have to do it again. The rule is that you will be home by the agreed upon time. Do you understand?" He answered yes, and we said goodnight and went to bed. No grounding and no shouting. He was rarely late after that.

> *If a child is assigned a purposeful ordeal or task as a consequence of misbehaving, he not only overcomes the misbehavior but learns something or accomplishes some good from the ordeal.*

Should something important come up that will delay your teenager's coming home on time, he needs to understand that he must call you before the designated hour to let you know he needs to extend the time. Otherwise, you will assume there is a problem and you will go find him. Keep in mind that to reinforce boundaries effectively you must be *kind, gentle, respectful,* and *firm*.

If his coming home late has become a habit that needs to be broken and you'd rather not go searching for him, you may want to establish a consequence—some ordeal that is unpleasant and has a good outcome. An ordeal is a task that is extremely inconvenient. It is not a punishment. Punishment has no good end in and of itself, whereas, if a child is assigned a purposeful ordeal or task as a consequence of misbehaving, he not only overcomes the misbehavior but learns something or accomplishes some good from the ordeal. An appropriate ordeal for the coming-home-late problem could be that he must wash, shine, and vacuum the car at 6:30 a.m. the next morning, and, so as not to disturb neighbors at that early hour, he may not turn on his music. The ordeal must be inconvenient and difficult enough to exceed the degree of disobedience.

Do not mention the ordeal earlier as a threat. If you let him know in advance what will happen if he is late, he may decide it will be worth the ordeal. After he arrives home late and you have listened to him with understanding, restate the rule about when he is to be home and then spring the ordeal on him: "I understand, and to help you remember the importance of being home at the agreed upon time, you are to wake up at 6:30 in the morning and wash, shine, and vacuum the car."

He may say, "Dad, not at 6:30! I'll do it later." Keep validating: "I know that's early and it will be tough; nevertheless, it must be done at 6:30 a.m." The inconvenient hour, as well as the labor, will make the impression. If he persists with, "Why so early?" just repeat your earlier statement, "This is to help you remember the importance of being home at the agreed upon time."

Punishment, such as grounding, rarely works. The ordeal of washing the car will accomplish something good—a clean car. Or, if you think this is not unpleasant enough for your son, you may think of an even better ordeal he can do. Just remember to validate his feelings, be *kind, gentle, respectful,* and *firm.* And always clearly restate the rule, i.e. "The rule is, you are to be home at twelve midnight."

At this point you may say to yourself, "But I don't want to get up at 6:30 myself to make sure it happens." That may be true, but believe me, the follow-through will allow you to have far more time of your own without the worry and frustration of your child's continued disobedience. And you will give him discipline that will help him develop into a responsible adult. It is a small price to pay for helping him learn responsibility and gain self-worth that lasts a lifetime.

Another father used the combined principles of validation and ordeal therapy on his son. He found a pornographic magazine in his son's room one evening when he was looking for a phone number. It surprised him because he had talked with his son about the dangers of pornography before. When his son came home that night he confronted him, showing him the magazine. The son became angry that his father had come into his room while he was gone. The father validated his anger with, "I understand your anger and I do respect your privacy. I didn't think you'd mind my looking for a phone number I thought you had. I didn't expect to run on to this. We'll talk about it tomorrow. Good night." Remember, nothing good

> *Remember, nothing good happens in the heat of the moment.*

happens in the heat of the moment.

The next morning, instead of going into a lecture on the evils of pornography, which his son already knew, he said to his son, "To help you get your fill of garbage I have arranged for you to pick up the trash in our local park. Here's the trash bag. Do it now and return when the bag is filled." The son said, "Dad, I don't want to pick up garbage." He replied, "I understand. It's an unpleasant job. Nevertheless, do it now." He took the bag and left, returning a few hours later with a bag full of garbage. The father thanked him. No lecture.

The next day the father handed his son the book *"As a Man Thinketh,"* by James Allen, and a tape recorder. He selected certain chapters and had his son go to his room and privately read aloud and record the chosen chapters. The father said, "That way I made sure he had read them." He said that seemed to be the end of his son's interest in pornography. Throughout the process he validated his son's feelings and followed through by being kind, gentle, respectful, and firm.

A mother of a teenage girl told of an incident when her daughter was tormenting her younger brother, pushing him around and even throwing a book at him. It was suggested that, after talking with the girl to discover her feelings about what was happening and validating those feelings, she could calmly and firmly state the family rule that we don't push, nor throw books at other family members. Then she could assign her daughter the ordeal of doing her younger brother's laundry, including washing, folding, ironing, and putting it away, for that week. This ordeal is a task with a good result directly relating to her brother. No sibling will want to do that more than once.

CONTROL YOURSELF

> *All the validating you do will be lost and meaningless if the conversation ends with a lecture.*

In every case I know of, validation has improved the relationship between parents and teenagers. There is a mistake some parents make as they begin to use validation. They think that after they have given their child the chance to express her feelings, and have validated those feelings, they can then bombard the child with a volley of verbal virtues. *That is not the time to teach.* If necessary, they may calmly restate family rules, but give no sermons. It must be remembered that all the validating you do will be lost and meaningless if the conversation ends with a lecture.

One mother reported her effort to try validation on her daughter. She said, "I was ready with a great validating phrase, but before I had a chance to use it on my daughter she sassed me. I was so angry at her for sassing that I snapped back at her, "Don't you talk to me that way, young lady!" The mother said she lost her desire to validate and wished only to punish.

Sassing is a method children use to throw you off guard and change the subject. Look beyond it. You must be in control of yourself. Validate the child's frustration. Then when the conversation about the initial problem is over, kindly and firmly say something like, "And never speak to me like that again." If you have been respectful and understanding of the underlying problem, she will likely apologize at that point for being disrespectful to you.

SILENCE CAN BE VALIDATING

Different validating approaches can be used for different situations. Loving silence, not just matter-of-fact or indifferent silence, but silence accompanied by a visible physical expression of concern, warmth, understanding and love can be highly effective. A good example of this is the following situation told by a father of a fifteen-year-old daughter:

My teenage daughter came into the house late one evening extremely upset. She ran upstairs and into her room, slammed the door, plunged on her bed and wept openly. I heard her crying through the door, stood helplessly by for several minutes, then decided to enter. I knocked quietly on the door, received an angry "What!" and asked if I could come in.   She angrily agreed. Fortunately, I decided that words were likely not appropriate, since she continued to sob uncontrollably.   I sat on the side of the bed beside her and gently placed my hand on hers. She cried on and on, then lay silent for several minutes, catching her breath with a sob here and there until she finally began to relax.

Then she began to tell me what had happened. She and her best friend had tried out for the high school tennis team and the tryouts came down to just the two of them. They were instructed to play a set against each other, the winner to be the last member of the team. They played nearby on the community-owned court and, since they were so evenly matched, the set went on and on with the game scores being tied again and again. After about two hours of hard and exasperating play, the other girl finally won.

To make matters worse, the girls, becoming increasingly exhausted and frustrated as they played, became angry with each other. Exhausted, humiliated, defeated, and terribly disappointed, she came home at about 11:00 p.m.

There were no words I could have said that would have been helpful. It was simply a bad experience that had to be suffered through. I said nothing about the ugly event. I just held her hand and listened, then, when my daughter was calm and ready for well-deserved sleep, I gently told her that I loved her and said goodnight.

My daughter continues to bring that experienc up and it is remembered now as a treasured moment between the two of us.

This father learned that, as hard as validating can be sometimes, a proper act of validation can take on a kind of life and permanence of its own, with both the validator and the person being validated forever enjoying the memory of it. Though caring silence can be effective in certain situations, often more is needed for our teenagers to feel validated.

THEY CAN MAKE WISE CHOICES

Teenagers need our expressions of confidence in their ability to think a problem through and make a wise choice. Get in the habit of saying, "What do you think?" Just don't slip and tell her what the wise choice is. That will almost always push her back into defending an unwise choice. If you have taught her through the years, those teachings and values are inside. She just needs a chance to think

> *If she can't come up with anything, try giving her a new way to look at the problem.*

about them and even challenge them. Most likely, if she is not forced by you into defending her thinking, she will be able to process the pros and cons and make better choices.

If she can't seem to come up with a possible solution, you may stimulate her thinking by giving her a different way to look at the situation. For example, she is telling you how hurt she felt today when her friend treated her rudely. After listening to her and validating her by saying something like, "That would hurt. If I were in your shoes I might have felt the same way." She may then say, "I just don't know what to do about it. What would you do?" You can say, "I'm not sure. What do you think could be done?" She might come back with something that is not good, such as, "I'd like to spit in her face!" No lectures on spitting in peoples' faces at this point will help. Just remember, she's expressing her feelings and you need to let her. You could say, "I can understand that's what you'd like to do." Sometimes just saying it puts it into perspective for her, and she may say, "But I can't do that." Then you ask again, "What can you do?" Each time you press for her to think of her own solution you must bite your tongue and refrain from telling her what she should do or what you would do. She must be given time to process her thoughts. This is one of those cases when silence is golden. This allows her to take her own responsibility for what needs to be done. She is the one facing the problem, not you. She was there, you weren't.

If she is really stumped and just can't come up with anything, try giving her a new way to look at the problem by saying, "Is there any difficultly going on in your friend's life right now that has nothing to do with you?" If there is, such as parents divorcing, illness in the family, or an important test she failed, your daughter can explore how that may have caused her friend to do what she did. If there is not, then you might offer a suggestion—not advice with "shoulds" or "oughts"—for handling the situation. Make it clear that it is only a suggestion that may or may not work and she may have a better idea. Following this process of validation, you empower your teenager by acknowledging her feelings, allowing her to consider options of her own.

With these thoughts in mind, consider again the scenario of the teenage daughter and her friends that was given in the introduction of this book:

My daughter said. "Mom, all they do is use me and treat me rude. They borrow my clothes, don't give them back when I want them, and when they give them back they're dirty." I knew the answer to her problem so I said, "Well honey, the answer is simple, just don't lend them your clothes and go get the ones they have and bring them home." She glared at me and said, "You just don't understand. You don't care. You never listen to me!" With that she ran out of the room. All I wanted to do was help her.

What would have made the outcome different? After the daughter complained about how her friends used her and her clothes, the mother could have said, "That hurts to be treated like that." Now she needs to pause and allow her daughter to process her feelings, her frustrations, and her sadness. Then the question could be asked, "What would you like to do?" The daughter will then likely come up with a solution that will work for her. She will likely thank her mom and leave in a much better mood.

Teenagers are intelligent people, and given the chance, they can come up with good ways to solve their own problems. The process of validation offers them the chance to think a problem through by talking about it freely without interruption, criticism, or lectures. When they don't have to defend their position because a parent is standing in the way of their thinking process, it is interesting to see what good ideas and solutions they can come up with. Allowing them this opportunity to develop problem-solving skills will go a long way toward helping them become responsible adults.

BEGIN TODAY

Start tonight by having a sit-down-together dinner with your family. This can be a nonthreatening setting that will create an atmosphere for conversation. Do not correct anyone's bad manners during the mealtime. Bring up a topic from the news that you think will be of interest to your teenager. Allow him the opportunity to respond in his own way without any criticism, no matter how off-base you may think his opinions are. Validate his comments with a phrase like, "Hmmm, that's an interesting thought." You do not have to agree with his opinion; just respectfully acknowledge it without judgment. Refrain from giving your own opinion at this time. Just listen and validate. Genuinely consider what he is saying.

If you do not try to change his way of thinking with your own ideas, he will continue opening up and sharing his true feelings about a subject. It may take a few times before he realizes you sincerely want to hear his point of view, but it will happen if you keep validating and trying to understand. It is only in this kind of atmosphere that he will begin to value your opinion.

Chapter Nine

How Validation Works With Adult Children

WE CANNOT CONTROL THEM

One of the hardest things for parents to realize is that when their children become adults they are no longer children. This realization is doubly difficult because they so often still act like children. Some of them don't handle their money well, some don't take care of their belongings, some end their marriage without even giving it a chance, some can't seem to hold a job, and the list goes on. We want them to grow up and take responsibility for their own lives and solve their own problems, and it seems inconceivable to think we are contributing to their *not* becoming responsible adults. All too often

> *Too often we are part of the problem.*

we are. The good thing about that is, if we are part of the problem, we have the power to control that part and change our approach once we recognize a better course.

In earlier chapters, when control was addressed, we established that we cannot control others—only ourselves. The phenomenal element of that truth is that when we make changes in our own behavior, others change in response to our change, without our saying anything about what changes they need to make. If we tell them to change, as we so often do, bad feelings result, and they don't change anyway. So why do we keep doing what doesn't work? All we can do as parents is change ourselves and our way of dealing with these *grown-up* children. That's where the magic of validation enters in.

When a grown child comes to you with a problem, don't immediately think they want you to solve it. Often they are just expressing their frustration and need to talk about it. Remember, everyone needs to feel that *I am of worth, my feelings matter, and someone cares about me.*

This is how a single twenty-six-year-old young woman put her disappointment about her parents' inability to validate her feelings:

I wish I could talk to my parents about

my frustrations. I want to get married, but I just haven't found a man that I love that much yet. If I say anything about it, my mother gives me this little speech about how I'm being too picky. Sometimes she even knows the "perfect" guy to set me up with. She's always trying to solve my problem, and that's not what I need. I wish she could just listen and understand without spouting off with some advice or trying to solve my problems.

A married couple told of their similar frustration over wanting to share feelings with a parent and not being able to do so. Here's their story:

When we had been married a few years, my widowed mother moved from her home nearly 2,000 miles away to the same city where we lived. She needed to be closer to family and we enjoyed having her nearby. She was well and able to care for herself and was quite independent. My wife liked her zest for life, but found it a little difficult to talk to her about some of our concerns.

Though well meaning, my mother seemed to feel that it was her responsibility to solve the problems we shared with her. My wife said to me one evening after speaking with her, "I wish she would just listen. I don't want her to solve anything. I just need a sympathetic, caring response with no advice attached." One particular conversation had to do with our lack of money at the time. Mother's response was, "I'm sorry, but I can't give you any money right now." My wife was a little hurt by the comment. She didn't want money; she just wanted someone to care enough to listen and be understanding.

The mother could have built a closer relationship with her daughter-in-law if she had responded with "That's a tough spot to be in. What are you going to do?" Talking about this problem was not a hint for their mother to give them some money, not even a hint to hear "Well, when Dad and I were young . . . ." The *when-I-was-young* sharing time can come later at a more appropriate time, and it definitely can be valuable information when given at the right time and the right time could be the next day. You could call her and say, "I've been thinking about our conversation and remembered an experience I had that was similar. . ." Given at the wrong time your experience can stand in the way. (See Chapter Six - *Find The Right Time To Teach*)

DON'T ALLOW THEM TO CONTROL YOU

On the other hand, sometimes grown children *do* talk to their parents about their financial difficulties

> If children any age
> continually "get"
> whenever they hint or
> ask for financial help,
> parents create a false
> economy for them.

with the express purpose of getting money. Both situations—when they're hoping for money and when they just want to talk—can be handled the same way. It helps immensely if you remember that *you do not have to make it all better.* In fact, you don't have the power to make it all better even if you give them the money. Often that will compound their dependency on you and create a feeling within them that they cannot make it on their own. That doesn't mean there isn't a time when parents can give financial help. What it means is: If children any age continually *get* whenever they hint or *ask* for financial help, parents create a false economy for them, an economy that says "ask and you get," instead of "work and you earn." Each person must keep their own responsibility and each must be *allowed* to keep it.

It is a safe guess that nearly every parent with a college student has had the I-need-more-money bomb dropped on them. Many parents have blown up when this bomb hit, completely losing their cool. In a voice befitting a seasoned army sergeant, they may have yelled something like, "I can't believe you've spent everything already! When are you going to learn a little responsibility?"

Because a child's main job in life seems to be to

get her needs met at all cost, a "No" is often followed by begging and sometimes accompanied by a few tears. This can happen even when they are adults. Some parents give in, send the money, and then resent it, feeling anger toward the child.

Consider this method of handling the situation. Your son calls home for money, and you know he had enough to handle his expenses when he left a few months earlier. Try validating his frustration by saying, "That's hard when the money runs out. I understand how that feels." He will likely reply, "It really is hard, and I don't know what I'm going to do." Keep validating, "That's a tough spot to be in." As you keep listening, his plea may start pulling at your heartstrings. You remember how fun it was during your own college days to have some extra money for dates, parties, clothes, and delivered pizza.

Then you hear, "Please, Dad. I won't ask for any more." You may be thinking, "Yeah, right." Don't say it; just keep on validating. "It would be nice to have some extra money. What do you think you could do to earn some?" Without getting angry, turn the problem back to him. Allowing him to solve his own problem could be as important a part of his education as the class work, maybe even more so. Let him know you love him and have confidence in his ability to solve his own problems.

What if he becomes angry at you and says, "I thought I could count on you, but obviously I can't!

Good-bye." Slam! Don't lose it here by calling him back. Remember, he is an adult and can find a way to earn some extra money. You don't need to solve his problem. If he doesn't blow up and hang up on you, you can even encourage him to think of ways he could earn some money. Don't tell him what he can do. Let him come up with the ideas. There are employment opportunities, such as tutoring, helping teachers correct papers, janitorial work, and flipping hamburgers at every college campus. Those who want and need the money badly enough will find a job and in so doing will develop even greater skills for coping and succeeding in life.

> *There is no need to make ourselves ill over our children's problems. All that does is complicate life even more than it already is.*

Parents often think their young adult children just can't make it on their own and worry themselves sick over it. If you took a good look at your feelings, you might discover that you are angry with your son for being so irresponsible with the money he already has. It is wasted energy and definitely unhealthy to foster this feeling. Remember, it can cause ulcers or other health problems. There is no need to make ourselves ill over our children's problems. All that does is complicate life even more than it already is. Realizing this, one father who discovered the value of validation, reported the following incident:

Our twenty-one-year-old married daughter and her husband lived in their own apartment in our same town. They had a six-month-old baby girl. Her husband did construction work and often had arguments with his boss, resulting in his getting fired more than once. Our daughter wanted to stay home and care for their baby, so she didn't have a job. Occasionally she would tend other children to bring in a little extra money.

Sometimes she would call us and say, "We don't have enough money to make our car payment. Could you loan us $200.00?" If we told her we didn't have the money she would say, "If you don't help us we'll lose our car and then we won't have any way to get to work to earn more money." We kept getting sucked in with this hard-luck story and somehow would find the money to loan them. It usually meant giving up something we needed ourselves. After doing this a few times and discovering that they would never pay us back, we became angry.

Once when we refused to loan her the money she said, "If you don't give us some money for food, don't plan on seeing your granddaughter ever again." We didn't give her any money then, but we did buy her some groceries.

After that incident we realized how we were allowing them to control us, and how irresponsible it was making them and how angry, even sick, it was making us. My stomach seemed to be continually upset and my wife's asthma worsened.

We let a few weeks pass, then, when things were cooled down, we went to visit them. My wife said, "We came to apologize. We've been treating you like children, and that's not fair to you. You are responsible adults and we're going to start treating you like it. In the past, we've been giving you money, as though you weren't capable of caring for yourselves. So, from now on we promise to treat you like adults." I added, "We won't be giving you any more money because we know you can take care of yourselves." We did it kindly, respectfully and firmly.

We had finally set our boundaries. We also told them that we would forgive any money they owed us in the past, and they could consider it a gift. We wanted to start with a clean slate.

They looked at each other, then to us, then her husband said, "That's right, we're adults and we can take care of ourselves from now on." Our daughter added, "Thanks for your help in the past. We'll be fine now."

After about two months our daughter called and said they were having another financial struggle. I said, "I'm sorry to hear that. What a difficult position to be in. We have confidence in you two and know you'll figure it out." We stuck to our guns and responded with understanding and empathy, but no money. Our anger dissolved, our health improved, and our relationship with them became more friendly. We invited them over for dinner occasionally, bought them gifts for birthdays and Christmas, and an outfit now and then for the baby, and that was it. They seemed to manage just fine without our money, having struggles from time to time, but they worked it out. It has taken time and courage, but now we're better friends with them than we've ever been.

> *Boundaries work best when both parents agree on and stick to them in a kind and respectful way.*

Notice how these parents finally drew their boundaries and continued to show their love through validation: "I'm sorry to hear that. What a difficult position to be in." They allowed their daughter and her husband to solve their own problems: "We have

confidence in you two and know you'll work it out."
This works best when both parents agree on the
boundary and stick to it in a kind and respectful way
as these parents did.

It seems to be a fact of life that when you owe
someone money or they owe you, the friendship dies.
It is no different with our children. These parents
could have set up a workable payment plan to have
their money paid back, but knowing the history of
difficulties their daughter and her husband had, they
decided to forgive the debt and start fresh. From that
point on they allowed them to be responsible for their
own lives.

When this approach is taken it gives parents the
freedom to become friends with their grown children
and share life with them on an adult level. Keep in
mind that this does not mean you never help them. It
just means you do it on *your terms*, judiciously, always
treating them with kindness and respect as you would
other adults. They need to know you will not be
manipulated by emotional outbreaks.

GIVE UP GIVING ADVICE

The temptation to tell our children what they
should do is ever present. When we look at their
situation we often think we have the answer to their
problem, and because we care about them, we want to
help them with our own ideas. It sounds good, but it
rarely works. One mother reported her discovery

regarding this. Here's her story:

> My twenty-nine-year-old son comes over to my house regularly and pours out all his frustrations about his girlfriend. He drives me nuts. I listen for awhile and then I always seem to end up saying, "How many times do I have to tell you to leave this girl? She's driving you crazy and me, too." Then he abruptly ends the conversation by jumping up and saying "Why can't you ever just listen!" and storms out the door.

> *My listening became invalidating when it ended with my advice.*

> I have prided myself in the fact that I always *do* listen to him. However, after learning about validation I realized that my listening became invalidating when it ended with my advice. So I made a change. The next time he came over and poured his frustrations out over his girlfriend, I really listened. I validated with, "That's got to be very difficult," and "Hmmm, I think I might feel the same if I were in your shoes." At no time did I give him any advice. He then began to formulate a plan that would be good for him. I was pleasantly surprised at what he came up with when I didn't tell him what to do.

It helps considerably if we remember that we have already taught our adult children most of what they need to know to succeed in life. For the most part, the time for our teaching them is past, though there are appropriate times to share ideas that may be helpful. (See Chapter Six - *Finding the Right Time to Teach*) If we are concerned that we may not have done a good job it helps to realize that we are not their only source of good information. Generally, given a chance, they will make some wise choices that fit their needs and situation. A mother of a young-married college-student son related the following story that illustrates this concept.

> Our son, Darren, and his wife, Susan, and baby came over one evening. They seemed down about something, and it didn't take long to find out what it was all about. Darren said, "That stupid car of ours is a piece of junk. We never know from one day to the next if it's even going to run." His wife chimed in, "We just spent three hundred dollars on repairs and it's still got some problems." My husband resisted saying, "You spent three hundred dollars on that piece of junk?" Instead he said, "Wow, that's got to be disappointing."
> "It's more than disappointing," Darren

said, "It's sickening! We need a new car."
He then went on to tell all about a great little
van he had seen and would love to have. This
was not the first time he had mentioned how
much he wanted a van. I said, "Wouldn't that
be great? I'll bet you'd really enjoy it. What
are you going to do?" I was dying to say,
"Don't even think about it. There's no way
you could afford it." And they really
couldn't. But I didn't say it. I can't tell you
how many times I had wished we had the
money to help make it happen for them, but
we didn't have it and they knew we didn't.
They weren't even hinting. They were just
sharing their frustrations with us.

Susan said, "We're not going to get a
van, but we do have to find a solution to this
problem soon." My husband said, "You two
are good at solving problems. I'm sure it will
work out." Then the conversation turned to
the baby.

A few weeks later Darren and Susan
came driving up in a "new" car. It was not a
van, but it was a good little used car. Susan
said, "Look what we found, and for only five
hundred dollars!" Darren was excited too
and said, "Can you believe it—and it works
great. It'll do until I get a real job and can
buy our van." We were amazed. That little
car has been purring right along for them for

several months now. I'm glad we didn't give
them a lot of advice. They might have taken
it and never found this great buy.

Another mother told of something she had
learned about validation that significantly helped her
in her relationship with her married daughter. The
daughter would call her mother sometimes when she
was angry with her husband. The mother often
thought the daughter's anger was not justified, or that
she was making too much out of nothing and
consequently was putting her marriage in danger. She
felt she had a responsibility to give her the advice that
might save her marriage. Here is her story:

I used to think I needed to calm my
daughter down and help her put the problem
in perspective. I would give her advice about
what she ought to do to solve the problem. It
never worked. She would always get madder
and then the anger would turn to me with
comments like, "You just don't understand."
or "Why do you always take his side? You
just don't get it!"
Now when she calls, I just validate her
feelings by saying something like, "That
would be hard," and she eventually calms
down and often even says, "I guess he's not so
bad after all. Maybe I should be a little more
patient with him." These are her words, not

mine.

By the time her husband comes home her frustrations are all gone and she is more in the mood to talk with him about her needs in a calm, respectful way. I think my learning how to validate her has not only saved my sanity and hers, it may even have helped save their marriage.

WHEN THEY BLAME YOU

Sometimes adult children will come back at their parents, complaining about material things or emotional support they feel they were deprived of when they were growing up. This often keys in defensive

> *You can't go back in time and make it all better, so just walk with him as he expresses his feelings.*

justification by the parents. An adult child referring to a younger sibling may say, "I never had half of what you give to Melissa." When this kind of statement is made, parents usually immediately defend themselves by saying, "We gave you all that we could at the time and you never went without the necessities." Or worse, you may be thinking what an ungrateful child he is and say, "How can you say that after all we did for you?"

Instead of that response, think how a little validation would work, like "I'll bet that was hard for you to go without so many things." No argument, just understanding. You can't go back in time and make it all better, so just walk with him as he expresses his feelings. With a little of this kind of understanding he will likely come around to saying something like, "I guess you have a little more money now than you did then." Or even, "Maybe I wasn't really too bad off. I had what I needed."

One example of being blamed for not giving the emotional support a child needed may come in the form of a statement such as: "You were never there for me. I can't even remember a time when you attended a school play or anything I was in." The common defensive reply is, "I wanted to, but it was impossible. You know very well I was working the night shift and could not get off." And she may reply, "Yeah, I know. Everything was more important than me." This leads to another defensive comment, "You *were* important to me. Why else would I work so hard trying to keep a roof over your head and meals on the table. You're an adult now. You should know all about how hard that is." All you have at this point is a good argument.

> *If you don't defend yourself and allow her to keep talking by validating her feelings, she will come around and finally let go of her harbored ill feelings against you.*

What validating comments might have been used instead? How about, "That must have been disappointing. I'm so sorry I missed out on that important part of your life." There is no need to defend your position. Let the child talk through her disappointments without standing in the way with your own justification. It is the only way she will get over it and come to peace with the situation. If you don't defend yourself and allow her to keep talking by validating her feelings, she will come around and finally let go of her harbored ill feelings against you.

One father told of an incident he had with his twenty-five-year-old son. They had had a confrontation and the son was extremely angry at his father. At one point the son said, "You never have treated me good." The father decided to stop defending and just listened. In an understanding tone he said only, "Oh." The boy went on, sobbing as he spoke, "I remember all those terrible spankings you gave me when I was little. They hurt me so bad. I didn't deserve that kind of abusive treatment." The father said it was tempting to stop him and say, "I never spanked you very hard, nor very often." But he didn't. He just listened and validated. When the boy was through the father said, "Thank you for sharing your feelings with me, son. I never realized you felt that way. I'm so sorry for what I may have done to hurt you. Please forgive me." The boy then calmly replied, "It's okay." The father embraced the boy and told him he loved him and the boy in turn said, "I love you, too, Dad."

Another graphic illustration of this came to my attention when a young adult woman told me she had been sexually abused by a neighbor when she was a child. She was still very angry at her mother for not protecting her from the neighbor, even though the mother did not know about the abuse at the time. It is normal for a child to expect to be protected by a parent. The young woman said, "My mother won't listen to me when I talk about it. She just says, 'I didn't even know it was happening. How can you be mad at me?' She just keeps defending herself."

During her next therapy session I had the mother come in with the young woman. At some point during the session I looked at the mother and said, "Did you ever sit on the edge of your bed and think 'How can I mess up my daughter today?' " She answered emphatically, "Of course not. I never consciously did anything to hurt her." I said, "I'm sure you didn't, and now that you and we know that, could you just sit here today and listen to her express her feelings?" She was more than willing—she was eager. I gave her some validating phrases to help her out, such as, "I'm so sad that happened," and "Oh, I wish I had known," and "I can understand your anger," and "I'm sorry."

After it was all out, the daughter and the mother both cried. The mother realized she did not need to defend her position. As the mother listened, the daughter felt validated and understood. Then the healing began. It was the very thing they both had been wanting.

BOOMERANG CHILDREN

There seems to be an epidemic of adult children returning home to live. Parents are usually not prepared for this, nor do they want it. However, when a daughter or son is having an especially difficult time due to divorce, job loss, illness, or other unfortunate circumstances, they often have nowhere else to turn. Sometimes they come home with their spouse and children as a temporary measure while they are waiting to move into a new home, until they graduate from college, or for some other reason. Whatever the reason for their return it can be difficult for both the parents and the returning adult child. The use of validation and the clear setting of parents' boundaries is imperative for this difficult situation to work without creating conflict and negative feelings.

The following story shows how one mother and father used these principles when their newly divorced son returned home to live.

Dave not only lost his wife, he also lost his job. He was devastated and so emotionally distraught he didn't know what to do. When he asked if he could come home for a time, my husband and I decided it could only work if we set some definite boundaries.

We loved him and wanted to help him, but knew if we didn't immediately establish some boundaries, he might take advantage of us and stay longer than it would do him or us any good. The boundaries were simple:
  (1) Keep all of your belongings in your room, and no spreading them out into the rest of the house.
  (2) Spend time each weekday looking for a job, and when that's finished, help out with chores around the house.
  (3) Do your own laundry.
  (4) Clean up whatever you mess up.
  (5) Be ready to move out into your own apartment in six months or sooner.

In a kind way we explained the boundaries to him. He understood and agreed to all of them.

Sometimes he would talk to me about his problems. Once, referring to his lost marriage he said, "I really messed up. I wish I had been a better husband. I don't know what I'm going to do." I was well aware that he had messed up and I found it difficult not to remind him of the mistakes he had made and tell him what I thought he should do. But I realized that would only make matters worse. Instead, I validated his feelings by saying, "What you're going through has got to be very difficult. What are you going to do?"

That seemed to open the way for him to fully express his feelings, and led him to say what he could have done, and what he was going to do about his life now. He needed to express his feelings and solve his own problems. Nothing I could say would make it all better anyway. By the sixth month he had found a new job and moved out. My husband and I both felt that he would have stayed much longer if we had not given him a deadline to work toward.

That was two years ago. He still has many emotional needs and now feels like he can call us and express those feelings since we won't tell him what to do. Knowing I don't have to solve his problems has taken a tremendous load off my shoulders. Now I can just listen and be more of a friend to him.

When boundaries are firmly understood by returning adult children, there is a greater chance of success in what might otherwise be a stressful situation. One thing I have said to parents in this situation is: Love them, *and don't make it too easy nor too comfortable for them.* If you do, it becomes too tempting for them to stay longer than is needful or

> *Love them and don't make it too easy nor too comfortable for them.*

good for them.   If your goal in allowing them to return is to help them on to greater success, then know that babying them along will not do it.   Give them responsibility while they are at home and a deadline for when they will be out on their own.   As you set your boundaries, it is imperative that you remember to be *kind, gentle, respectful,* and *firm,* and, in all cases, validate their feelings.

WHEN THEIR LIFESTYLES DON'T MATCH YOURS

Don't we all wish our children would take the good from our lives and emulate it?   When we teach them principles of moral responsibility we hope and pray that they will adhere to these teachings and pass them on to their own children.   It doesn't always happen that way.   So what do you do when it doesn't happen?   As they talk to you about their frustrations, it can be extremely difficult to refrain from telling them how they need to change their lives. You have a dozen sermons on the tip of your tongue, and I suggest you hold them and just listen and validate their feelings. If you remember that advice doesn't work, it will free you up to listen in a way that shows genuine caring and love.

Many parents who display this depth of love and understanding with their children who choose undesirable lifestyles, later experience the joy of seeing them return to what they were taught as young children.

One woman whose grown daughter has abandoned their family's basic religious principles said, "I found out that no amount of preaching brings her back to my way of thinking. It only stops her from communicating with me. I finally realized that if she is ever going to return to these basic principles she'll have to do it her way and in her time. In the meantime I can show her my love by listening and not criticizing her." This is an important discovery. Even if her daughter never does return to become a practicing member of their church, everyone in the family will be happier because of the love and acceptance she has been given.

Many parents who display this depth of love and understanding with their children who choose undesirable lifestyles, later experience the joy of seeing them return to what they were taught as young children. It may take years in some cases, but I have seen it happen enough times to encourage people to hold on with hope and just keep loving that child. Remember, at no time does this kind of love mean you give up your own values. It just means you cannot force them on your grown children.

One poignant example of this happened to a couple whose son had drifted away from the teachings of his youth, gotten his girlfriend pregnant, married her, had children, but would not embrace the religious beliefs he had been taught in his childhood and youth. Later he became involved with another woman, but felt terrible about it and tried to put his marriage back together. He even seemed to succeed for a time. Off and on throughout this period his parents tried to help him realize that his life would be better if he would return to his religious upbringing. At one point he angrily told them, "Don't ever speak to me about religion again. I don't want anything to do with it."

A few years later the son's wife had an affair and divorced him. This was the lowest point in his life and he began to threaten suicide. It was then that his father called me and asked what he could do. He said, "I've told him over and over that he needs to get on with his life and just put the past behind. And I didn't even mention religion to him. Still he talks only of suicide. What should I do?"

I said, "I won't tell you what you 'should' do, but I have a suggestion you might try. See what happens when you stop trying to solve his problems by telling him what to do *and just let him talk*. Validate his sadness and loss. Walk with him and let him feel what he is feeling." I gave him some validating phrases he could try. Because he was a religious man I suggested he could pour his frustrations out in prayer since he would no longer be pouring them out on his son.

A few weeks later he called me back and said, "It's amazing what happened after I stopped telling my son what to do and just validated him. I mean it was amazing! At that point he seemed to start coming back to reality. Now he is back to work and doing quite well." Several weeks after that I was told that his son had begun dating a woman he had known for a few years at work. She believed in him and they were planning a wedding. He said, "Dad, I want you to speak at our wedding. And you can say anything you want, and I really mean anything . . . even religious. My fiance and I are going to church together now and I have never been happier."

This man continues to express gratitude for learning how to stop trying to solve his son's problems and start validating him instead. I earnestly suggest this to all parents in similar situations. It will take the heavy responsibility of trying to solve a child's problem off of your shoulders and place it where it belongs—on his. That's when it becomes possible for good things to happen.

THE UNIVERSAL NEED

As you deal with your adult children, it helps to keep in mind the universal need of all people: *I am of worth, my feelings matter, and someone really cares about me.* Understanding the importance of this need will help you use the principles of validation in all of your communication with them. It will also help you set boundaries that will not only help them but will remind you that you, too, are of worth and your feelings matter.

BEGIN TODAY

Call one of your adult children today and ask how things are; then just listen. Use some of the validating phrases and resist giving any advice to her. If she tells you about a problem and if she asks you what she should do about it, validate her frustrations and, under no circumstances, give her a solution. Instead, turn it back to her and ask her what she thinks would work or use other appropriate questions from chapter six to stimulate her thinking.

As you continue this she will begin to realize you value her opinion and that the responsibility for her problem lies within herself.

After the conversation, hang up and pat yourself on the back for a job well done. You will be well on the way to empowering your child to solve her own problems in the way that is best for her and a greater friendship between the two of you will begin to blossom.

Chapter Ten

—·····—

How Validation Works With A Spouse

WHAT GETS IN THE WAY?

Because our spouse is the most important person in our life we have an intense desire to heal any hurts and make any wrongs right for her (or him). We want the best for our spouse and too often do everything in our power to make things all better for her. In fact, we feel duty bound to

> *The lack of validation can cause our spouse to lose self-esteem and diminish feelings of romantic love.*

do it. This is what gets in the way of validating the one person we love more than anyone else, and we usually end up creating a greater problem for them rather than solving one. The lack of validation can also cause our spouse to lose self-esteem and diminish feelings of romantic love for us.

Take, for instance, the wife who feels sad and upset about her weight problem. She may say to her husband, "I don't know why I can't get this weight off. It's been nearly a year since the baby was born, and it's still hanging on." Her husband doesn't realize she is simply communicating her feelings and needs validating. His perception is, she has a problem and he is going to help her solve it, so he says, "Maybe if you would eat a little less and exercise a little more." Is that what she needs to hear? Absolutely not. She already knows that. What does she need to hear from him that would help her more than anything? How about if he gave her his full attention, gently validated her feelings with, "That's got to be discouraging, honey," and then listened as she poured out her disappointments and frustrations.

At some point, *if* he continues to validate her, she will come up with her own plan of action to lose the weight. At that point he may ask her if there's anything he can do to help with her plan. She may say, "No. I'll work it out." Or, "Yes, could you watch the baby while I exercise?" It's got to be her plan, her idea, or it won't work, no matter how magnificently he states his advice. Also, by enthusiastically jumping on her band wagon, he may make her feel he doesn't love her the way she is. When that worry is added to her own concerns, then the problem becomes twice as difficult to work on.

One of my clients had this problem. He was

worried about his wife's weight, and kept encouraging her to do something about it. His comments never did anything but cause ill feelings between them, and seemed to prevent her from doing anything about the problem. After finding more peace in his own life, he handled the situation differently. Here's his report:

I realized how much I loved my wife and decided to stop saying anything about her weight and just express my love for her every day. A few weeks after I had been doing that I noticed she got some information in the mail on how to lose weight. I said to her, "Honey, my fear is that you're doing this for me because I pushed you before. You don't need to lose any weight for me. I love you just the way you are." And I meant it. She said, "That's what makes it possible for me to do it. I'm not doing it for you—I'm doing it for me." And she really seemed excited about it.

Too often we think we must do something to help our mates solve their problem or they just won't do it. Believe me, our pushing will only make it worse. Understanding is what is needed. Most of us are too impatient with our mates. We may think, "Why can't he see it? It is so obvious what needs to be done." or, "It's a waste of energy for her to spend so much emotion over such a small thing." Time, patience, love, listening, and understanding can help heal and solve most problems within a marriage. We have chosen to walk beside our mate in life's problems, and learning how to walk emotionally beside each other can build a unity that will allow us to discuss and resolve any difficulties we may face. It really doesn't take much time to do it right in the beginning. It just takes a little know-how and remembering that we each need to feel that *I am of worth, my feelings matter, and someone really cares.*

WHAT TO DO ABOUT A NO GOOD VERY BAD DAY

I think everyone can relate to Judith Viorst's children's book, *Alexander and the Terrible Horrible No Good Very Bad Day.* We all have them. Consider the following scenes between spouses:

Scene I - **Husband:** you come home from work and find your wife looking pale and exhausted, like she has just finished the Boston Marathon, and definitely did not win. You ask the magic question, which is not "What's for dinner?" The magic question is, "How was your day, honey?"

Scene II - **Wife:** you see your husband open the door dragging his briefcase about six feet behind him, looking sad and dejected. You ask him the magic question, "How was your day, honey?"

Now take a moment and think how you would feel if, after you have shared the happenings and frustrations of your day, your spouse said something like: "Well, dear, if you were just a little more organized your day would have gone much better."

> *It is important to be able to freely express what is going on inside of you to a listening and caring person without fear of criticism.*

This may be one of those times when you feel a combination of emotions— *mad* and *afraid*. Mad because you are being criticized and not understood. Afraid because you have an urge to do bodily harm to your spouse.

What *is* needed after a bad day? Isn't your main desire just simply to be heard? Then listen as he tells you what went on during his day. Do not try to explain away the problems of his day. JUST LISTEN! Let him express his frustrations, his anger, or whatever he needs to say. Listen for his needs. You don't need anyone to solve anything for you, or to tell you how to do things better. It is important to be able to freely express what is going on inside of you to a listening and caring person without fear of criticism, and there is no better person to fill that role than your spouse. This kind of sharing defuses anger, relieves frustration and confusion, relaxes tension, and builds a loving relationship.

One husband said, "But when I come home,

I'm tired. I work all day and I don't need to hear all these problems." He is afraid that by hearing them, he has to fix them. All he needs to do is listen and validate, not solve. Just listening will end up fixing it far more than anything he may tell her she "ought" to do or "should" have done.

Putting emotions and thoughts into words will often bring order to what might have been confusion. At that point, the person's view of what happened often changes, giving her a different perspective of the events. If there was a problem to be solved, this fresh perspective allows the discovery of a possible solution to come from within her. I have often had the experience of someone coming to my office and in the process of explaining his problem (during which I listen intently and ask a few questions), he has come up with an excellent solution. Then he has said, "Thank you so much for the answer to my problem. You have done so much." In reality all I did was validate his feelings and ask a few questions.

A friend of ours experienced a terribly hectic day that she won't soon forget. As owner of her own business, she was frantically hurrying, trying to accomplish several days worth of work in one day because she and her husband would be leaving for a week's vacation. He was busy at his own job and couldn't be of much help. One of the have-to's on her list was to make a tax deposit at the bank which had a deadline of 3:00 p.m. Her accountant had not explained the complexity of it to her, so she thought it would be a simple five-minute task at the teller window. She barely made it to the bank in time, only to discover that she had to open a whole new account at the new accounts desk. After a great deal of frustration, she completed the task thirty minutes past the deadline. By the time she got home she was exhausted physically and emotionally.

As she recounted her frustrating day to her husband, he said, "You should have known you would have to open a new account. Anybody knows that." She was infuriated by his response. (They had attended one of our seminars several months earlier where they first learned about validation.) She said, "I felt like decking him! But I didn't. Instead, I said, 'Why couldn't you just validate my feelings and say you're sorry I had such a bad time instead of making me feel like an idiot for not knowing?' " He said, "Oh, *that's* how validation works. Now I get it." She said, "I think we've had a major breakthrough."

HANDLING DISAPPOINTMENT

Disappointments are generally due to some kind of loss, such as a job, a friendship, a valuable possession, etc. No matter how large or small the disappointment, there is a feeling of sadness at not getting something you wanted or losing something you valued. Being free to feel and express these feelings helps resolve the loss, as was the case in the following experience reported by a writer:

> I was expecting to receive a choice assignment. I told my husband all about it and how much this writing opportunity would mean to me. He was hopeful with me as I anxiously awaited the confirmation. The call came and to my great disappointment, the assignment was given to another. I could not hold back the tears and was crying when my husband came home. He said, "What happened?" When I told him he said, "Oh, no! I know how much that meant to you. I'm so sorry." He then put his arms around me and held me close. We sat on the couch and he just let me cry and tell all about my disappointment.
>
> I am so glad my husband didn't say, "Cheer up, honey. You're a good writer and I'm sure you'll get many other opportunities." Instead he just held me as I cried and talked about my lost opportunity. After a few minutes I stopped crying, and looked up at him and said, "It's okay. I'm sure I'll get other opportunities." Then he enthusiastically said, "You bet you will.

PMA statements are most effective when they follow your spouse's own positive statements.

You're a darn good writer." Though I was
still disappointed, I didn't feel near the
sorrow after that. I felt ready to move on to
something else.

Her husband walked with her where she
needed to go and didn't try to change her. With his
validation she was able to bring herself back up to a
positive level. Then he validated her positive
statement with an appropriate PMA statement of his
own. PMA statements are most effective when they
follow your spouse's own positive statements. In fact,
a PMA at that time validates the spouse. Keep in
mind, validation is walking beside the other person
emotionally in what she is feeling.

Consider what might have been done in this
next experience told on a TV talk show by a woman
whose dear friend had died. She missed her friend
terribly. After hearing the news, she said she laid in
bed that night still crying. Her grief was so intense she
couldn't stop. At some point her husband said,
"You've got to stop crying. Life goes on. You've got
to get over it and get on with your life." She said to
the show host, "Where's the affection and caring?"

What did this woman need? Isn't it a loving
embrace with a simple validation, such as, "I'm so
sorry it happened. I know how much she meant to
you." (The apostle Paul gave the Romans good
counsel for just such an occasion when he said, "Weep

with them that weep.")[14] This husband could have then given her a listening ear as she talked about her friend.   Remembering the four rules of validations—LISTEN, LISTEN, LISTEN, and try to UNDERSTAND—can help us through any difficult situation.

Before departing on a trip one evening, my wife was browsing in the airport gift shop and couldn't help overhearing a conversation between a couple in their early sixties regarding his having forgotten his sunglasses. As she picked up on the conversation she heard the wife say to her husband, "That was such a stupid thing to do. Now you'll have to buy new ones." Defensively he said, "I didn't mean to leave them." Angrily she retorted, "I don't know how you could have. They were sitting right there on the table." He said nothing. Then she said, "Well, you can't go on the trip without sunglasses." Then, with a sigh of disgust, she added, "We'll just have to buy new ones." Without saying another word, he picked out a new pair, paid for them, and they left with enough negative electricity between them to cause a power outage.

Can you see how simple and how different the whole situation could have been had she just validated her husband's feelings by saying something gentle like, "I'm sorry you forgot your

> As soon as we start defending we invite an argument.

sunglasses. What would you like to do?" That kind of validating comment shows love and respect. Then he is free to make a decision in a pleasant atmosphere and the trip isn't ruined with underlying anger. Nothing is ever gained by humiliating your spouse. More importantly, a whole lot of love can be lost.

STOP DEFENDING YOUR POSITION

Sometimes when our mates are unhappy about something we have done that hurts them and they're expressing their feelings to us about it, we think we have to defend ourselves. As soon as we start defending we invite an argument. An example of this happened in a therapy session in my office. The wife said, "He never remembers my birthday, our anniversary or even Christmas." The husband justified himself with, "I never have enough money to buy gifts." She said, "I don't need gifts. All I need is to be remembered."

I suggested they stop right there and had them both do a little validating instead of trying to defend their own positions. I gave them a few validating phrases to try, and had them start over. After the wife again told of her sadness at not being remembered by him on special days, he, with a little coaching, gently responded with, "I understand you're disappointed, and I'm really sorry. I didn't realize how important that was to you." Then when he explained his reason, "lack of money," she validated him by saying, "I know it is difficult when you want to buy something and there's not enough money. I didn't know you wanted to buy me anything." From that point on they talked about her need to be remembered and how he could meet that need through cards or tender expressions of love on those special occasions. *Validation always opens the door to communication, and the lack of validation always closes it.*

What about the wife who says to her husband, as she's sitting at the table writing out the bills, "We just don't have enough money to pay all these bills." Too often his loud response is, "I work my tail off trying to bring in enough money! What do you expect me to do?" And too often her angry response to him is, "Hey, don't get mad at me. I work my tail off, too, and I don't see you sitting here trying to make ends meet." Now we've got a battle going.

What do you think would happen to the conversation if, after his wife's first statement, the husband validated her frustration with, "That's got to be hard, honey. I sure appreciate how hard you try. I wonder if there's anything else we could do." Then, in a spirit of respectful cooperation they might consider some options. By validating her frustration instead of defending his

> *You teach your mate how to use validation by using it yourself as often as possible.*

position, there are no bad feelings and no argument. This same result could be achieved if after the husband's statement "I work my tail off to bring in enough money. What do you expect me to do?" the wife could ignore his anger and validate him instead of defending her position. The argument could be defused through the use of a validating statement such as, "You really do work hard and I appreciate all you do. Maybe together we could figure out what to do here." Regarding finances, the only thing worse than not having enough money is fighting over not having enough money.

After the principle of validation is learned we sometimes get disgusted with our mate because he or she didn't use it. We seem to think it is the other person's job. It is important to remember that we cannot control what anyone else says. We can only control what *we* say. It is fascinating to observe what can happen when, at any point during a conversation, you start validating your spouse's feelings. The arguing will stop immediately and effective solutions can then begin to be worked out. You teach your mate how to use validation by using it yourself as often as possible.

DO IT OVER

It takes practice to become proficient at most good habits, and validation is no exception. We all make mistakes as we learn and it is important to remember that we can do it over. One young wife told the following experience of how she did it over:

>My husband called me from work and complained about his boss's unfair treatment of him. The fear of a lost paycheck reared its ugly head and I said, "Don't do anything about it because you might lose your job and then what would we do?" That brought the conversation to a halt and he said good-bye. As I thought about it and how I could have validated his frustrations I decided to call him back and do it over.
>
>When I had him on the phone again I said, "I've been thinking about your problem with your boss and decided it must be very frustrating to have to work there every night with her. That's got to be difficult, and I want to thank you for all your hard work." Then I just listened. I could not believe how quickly he responded. He told me that he appreciated me calling him back and that he had already written his boss a note in defense of himself. As he told me this I was thinking to myself, "Oh, no. He shouldn't have done that," but I didn't say anything about that

> If you don't validate at first, you can back up and do it over.

thought. Instead, I told him that since he was the one there, not me, he would be the one to know what was best, and if that didn't work he could always try something else. Then the best thing of all happened—he told me what a great wife I was and how much he appreciated my support. Things not only improved at work after that, they improved at home as well.

Keep in mind that if you don't validate at first, you can back up and do it over. Your spouse will only respect and love you more for the effort and understanding.

Another young wife was frustrated over the way her college-student husband had procrastinated finishing a correspondence course necessary for graduation. She said, "I was so irritated at how he was putting it off. He kept saying to me, 'I'm not going to meet the deadline. I'm so busy with my regular classes that I just don't have time. I guess I'll have to graduate next semester.' " She was very upset by this comment because they had used up all their extensions and it would cost them $500 to take the course again. She was angry at him and said, "If you had done it before this semester like you said you would you would not be in this bind now."

He was so angry at her for not understanding

the pressure he was under that he walked out and slammed the door. She said, "I realized I had handled it all wrong and decided I needed to validate him." When he returned she said to him, "Honey, I'm sorry. I know you're really working hard and it's difficult to get everything done. Is there anything I can do to help you so you can graduate on time?" He appreciated her understanding and the two of them worked out a plan that made it possible. She said, "Every time I validate his feelings and try to understand from his perspective, things go so much better."

This is another good example of how you can do it over when you have forgotten to use validation in the first place. It's never too late.

THE MALE AND FEMALE DIFFERENCE

> *By interrupting him she pushes away the very thing she is after——genuine communication with her husband.*

In using validation it will also help to understand the differences between men and women regarding the communication of feelings. Women generally come equipped with the ability to verbalize their feelings with much greater ease than men. According to one study, "Women are better at almost all the skills that involve words (fluency, verbal reasoning, written prose and reading). A woman's memory of words and language is also better."[15] This ability is an advantage that comes with a built-in disadvantage if women are not careful. For example, a woman's mind often races ahead of what her husband is saying. At times she will even finish his sentences for him and even be quite accurate. However, he will feel devalued because she has not allowed him to finish verbalizing his own thoughts.

It is vitally important for a woman to validate a man by letting him finish expressing his thoughts *at his own pace and without interruption.* By interrupting him she pushes away the very thing she is after—genuine communication with her husband. If a wife does not allow her husband to communicate without interruption, it can, and often does, cause rage inside of him, even though he may not exhibit the rage at the time. It may come out later in the form of ulcers or abuse.

A woman will likewise experience tremendous frustration if her husband does not allow her to finish expressing her feelings. Sometimes men interrupt this process with a comment like, "Hey, things aren't that bad." She must be allowed to feel that they *are* that bad, and in so doing she will be able to go to the emotional depth she needs to and then work back up to a more positive feeling.

It helps considerably if a woman realizes she must give a man time to mull things over. Moments of silence can be a valuable part of their conversation. Dr. John Gray, in his book *Men Are From Mars,*

Women Are From Venus, points out that women "think out loud, sharing their process of inner discovery," while men "internally and silently figure out the most correct or useful response."[16]   If a man is not allowed time to process information, he will likely have an angry reaction. Once you realize this difference, you will recognize the value of both processes. One is not better than the other; they are just different. Knowing this will help you listen with greater understanding and enable you to validate your mate more effectively.

SETTING FAMILY VALUES

It is extremely helpful in a marriage if the couple openly discuss their feelings about family values. Values differ according to a person's family of origin. Each will come into the marriage having been taught differing points of view regarding certain values. Even if they have the same basic values, they may have differing degrees of adherence to a particular value. It is important for them to decide what values they want to have in their marriage and with their own growing family.

One young couple was struggling with this. The wife felt strongly that it was destructive to their family to view sexually explicit or brutally violent movies and videos. The more she preached to her husband about the evils of these things, the more he felt driven to watch them. She also noticed the lack of respect he showed for her after viewing films like these. She knew he had been taught by his parents that such videos were not desirable.

After learning about validation, she decided to try it. The next time they were at a video shop choosing a movie, he headed for the more explicit ones. Instead of her usual sermon, she followed him and said nothing as he picked up and read about some possible movies. When he said, "I'd like to see this one," her response was, "I understand. It looks interesting. I just wish they wouldn't put so much garbage in it. It could be such a good movie without it." No sermon. Just validation without attacking him or his value system. He said, "Yeah," and put the video back. They went on without argument to find one a little closer to what they would both enjoy.

> *A lot of conflict will be eliminated if a couple would sit down together and decide on their own family values.*

Validating never means giving up your own value system. It means you are trying to understand the other person's point of view while you stand firm with your own boundaries. Peace in marriage will be attained if boundaries are set by being kind, gentle, respectful, and firm. If you leave out kind, gentle, and respectful, then "firm" won't have a leg to stand on.

A lot of conflict will be eliminated if a couple,

at a time out of the heat of the moment, sit down together and decide on their own family values. These values could include principles of honesty to each other and others, commitment to marriage, methods of disciplining their children, religious activity, relationships with extended family members, commitments to jobs, the kind of movies they watch, and other matters that affect their boundaries and values.

ENJOY EACH OTHER'S DREAMS

It is interesting to observe how some spouses relate to each other when one wants something that is out of the question. For example, consider the husband who is a died-in-the-wool football fan. His favorite team makes it to the Super Bowl and he (knowing there is no way he can miss work or even afford the trip), says to his wife, "Oh, man would I love to go to the Super Bowl." Feeling afraid that if she validates his feelings he might take it as an okay to go, she says, "There's no way we can afford it." She somehow forgets that he already knows that. Think how he would feel if she said instead, "That would be so fun for you. I wish it were possible." Likely his response will be, "That would be fun, but oh, well, I guess they'll have to win without me there." She might even want to understand his need further and suggest, "Would you like to invite some friends over and we'll have pizza and watch the game here?" How do you think he would feel toward her with this understanding approach?

How about the wife who says to her husband, "I saw this beautiful new couch that would look so gorgeous in our living room." This kind of a comment can panic some men who know there is no money for such a purchase, and they might respond with, "Our old couch is just fine, and anyway we don't have any money for new furniture, so why were you even looking?" Think how she might feel toward him if he responded instead with, "That would be neat to get a new couch and someday we're going to. What did it look like?" And then let her express her feelings about it. After she tells all about it and expresses how much she would like a new couch, she will likely say, "But I know we can't get it yet." He might then go on to suggest that they consider together a special "Couch Fund" to help set aside the extra money needed for such a large purchase.

It is fun to follow a dream with your mate, even though you both know it can't happen yet. Someday it just may happen and in the meantime, validating those feelings and being able to share those dreams with each other, even if they never do materialize, feels so good. You don't need to try to talk each other out of anything. Often, just by being able to

> *I don't think people fall out of love, I believe they forget to love their spouse.*

share these feelings with a spouse, the person talks him or herself out of it.

PLAN TIMES TOGETHER

With the hectic pace of life and the many demands that seem to grab the time of each spouse, the marriage relationship often gets lost. There must be overt action taken by each to keep the romance alive and important. I almost hear some of you saying, "But where do I find that extra time to do that? My children (and/or business) demand so much time there is none left." I have heard some people say they have just fallen out of love. I don't think people fall out of love, I believe they *forget* to love their spouse. They forget the importance of making time for each other and they drift apart. They forget the importance of making their mate number one.

When a mate does not feel like number one, the seeds are sown that generally grow into divorce. Often that mate feels lonely and neglected and may turn to someone else for understanding. If you think it is tough now to find the time to build a strong marriage, the challenge of remarriage and blending families make this infinitely more difficult. The demands on time are spread to more people and the feelings of guilt complicate what

> *Setting the stage for times when you can be alone to share intimate feelings will not just happen.*

you do. It is well worth taking the time to build what you have now. Leo Weidner in his book, *Achieving the Balance*, puts it this way:

> So many marriages end up where the couples are actually married singles, because the spark of excitement that was there in the early days is hardly a flicker now. Couples create separate lives for themselves while remaining married. It doesn't have to be this way if both partners make a sincere effort to spend time attending to each other, asking how they can be a better partner and listening.[17]

Setting the stage for times when you can be alone to share intimate feelings will not just happen. These times must be planned for and made to happen. Weidner makes a plea to set aside a definite time for a date night—a night that each mate can count on. My wife and I have adhered to this for many years and have chosen Friday night. When our children were very young or finances were tight, we had to be creative in making time to be together. Sometimes we could be gone for only a short time or couldn't afford a babysitter, dinner, and a movie. We would choose to go for an hour alone and talk over a soft drink or a yogurt. The important thing for us was just being *alone together*.

When our children were older we would go on

an overnight trip to the big city forty miles away, get a motel room, have dinner, and walk hand-in-hand without having to meet any schedule. We would share our feelings, desires, and dreams. We could do this because we had the time together without anybody, any phone, or any schedule demanding our attention. These are very romantic and intimate times that have kept our love alive and fun. We highly recommend it. Being together like this provides an ideal opportunity for listening and validating each other. In fact, if listening and validating do not take place during these get-aways, the experience will not be as rewarding and fulfilling as it could be.

SENSE EACH OTHER'S NEEDS

> *Validation can come in the form of a little tender loving care.*

Many of our needs go unspoken because we don't know how to express them, even when we feel safe doing it. Other times we are hardly aware of what we need. That's when validation can come in the form of a little tender loving care. Here's an example from my own life that illustrates the point. After a particularly heavy session of therapy with a couple threatening divorce, I sat at home in my study pondering the situation. My wife came in, took one look at me and seemed to know what I needed. She said, "How would you like a good neck and shoulder massage?" And she began giving me one even before I answered because she knows how much I enjoy it. As she massaged, I began to express my frustrations. She didn't say much, just continued massaging and validating with phrases like, "Oh," and "Hmmm, that's a tough one." At one point she even said, "I think you're amazing." I wasn't feeling very amazing; however her comment reminded me of a favorite Kenny Rogers' song, *She Believes In Me,* and it felt so good.

On the other hand, sometimes when I see that my wife is frustrated, I've found that she just needs to be held and listened to. Other times I find that I need to roll up my sleeves and help with some household tasks. When I respond to that need the result is always positive. In our earlier years of marriage we were not this sensitive to each other's needs. We wish we had understood this principle years ago because it has brought so much happiness into our marriage.

A professor at a nearby university enjoyed the closeness this type of validation brought to his marriage. Here's his story:

One evening, several years ago, I was feeling the pressure of an important work assignment. After dinner I decided to return to work, as I had been doing quite regularly. As I departed, I noticed my wife alone in the kitchen standing over a hot stove processing and bottling several batches of fresh grape juice.

Half way to campus I suddenly had the urge to go back home. I turned the car around and headed back, parked, and walked into the house to my wife's surprise. She said, "What happened? Did you run out of gas?" I replied, "No. I decided it was more important for me to be here helping you make the grape juice." I put on an apron, asked what I could do and then pitched in. After a few minutes I noticed there were tears in her eyes. We shared a memorable evening bottling juice, visiting and sharing ideas in a way we hadn't for some time.

> *The greatest gift you can give your children is parents who love each other.*

Tuning in to our mate's needs, then validating and asking how we can help meet those needs, does wonders to build peace and joy into marriage. We must not assume we know *all* the needs of our spouse and that we have *all* the right answers to her or his problems. It is important to remember that *we don't have to make everything all better, and, in fact, we don't even have the power to make everything all better.* However, we can show greater love by listening, understanding, and offering our help. In so doing, we empower our mate to come up with his or her own best solutions. When this is done on a regular basis, feelings of romantic love increase and couples experience deep fulfillment and joy in their marriage. Your children will notice the love you have for each other and it will give them a great sense of security. I firmly believe that the greatest gift you can give your children is parents who love each other.

BEGIN TODAY

Today is the perfect day to begin validating your spouse. When you are with him (or her) this evening ask him how his day went. Then just listen and validate his comments. If it was good, be happy with him by saying something like "I'm really happy that happened. How did you feel?" Then listen and let him enjoy the fun of sharing with someone who really cares. If it was frustrating, ask him what happened and just listen without trying to talk him out of his feelings.

If he says, "I'd rather not talk about it right now," then validate that feeling and don't push him. Sometimes we would like to forget about unpleasant things for a while. If he feels you understand that, the chances are he will open up to you later and share his feelings. When he does, just listen and validate, and under no circumstances try to change his thinking or give him a solution. Try it tonight and see what happens. If you continue validating him, he will begin opening up to you and a much closer relationship will develop.

Chapter Eleven

---·•●•·---

How Validation Works With Parents And Parents-In-Law

LET THEM HAVE THEIR FEELINGS

In many families there is a lot of conflict between grown children and their parents, and sometimes even more with parents-in-law. Too many of us are so used to defending our own position and being irritated by their telling us what to do that validating their feelings doesn't even occur to us. We think they should be the ones validating ours—after all, *they* are the parents. The problem is, if they don't know how to do it, then it is not going to happen. When we remember that the only person we can control in life is ourself, then we can relax and begin controlling ourselves by validating them. And it is remarkable what happens when we do.

To illustrate, consider the following example: You are having a conversation with your mother, telling her about a new job opportunity that will require you to move to a new location. She has enjoyed

> *She cannot be sincerely excited and happy for you until her feelings have been validated.*

having you live in the same town as she and isn't at all excited about losing that close association. She may say, "Oh, no. I don't want you to move." The usual comeback is, "Mother, don't you understand what a great opportunity this is for me? You should be excited about it, too." It doesn't work to tell her what she "should" be feeling. It is important to remember that she cannot be sincerely excited and happy for you until her feelings have been validated.

So instead you might say, "I think I understand how you feel, Mother. It's been so nice living near you, and I will really miss that, too." At this point don't add any "buts" like, "but this is a great opportunity for me." She needs to be the one to say that to you and she probably will if you don't try to talk her out of her feelings. Remember the four rules of validation: LISTEN, LISTEN, LISTEN, AND UNDERSTAND.

Giving her a chance to express what she is feeling will allow her to go to the depth of her emotions that she needs to go. If you don't stand in the way of this process she will come full circle and be able to see what an important career opportunity this is for you. Then as you talk about your excitement over your promotion she will be able to enjoy your happiness with you. The door will be open then to freely talk about your new assignment and even plan the fun visits and phone calls you both will make, assuring her that you will keep in close touch.

DON'T TRY TO CHANGE THEIR THINKING

Validating parents' feelings allows them to solve their own problem regarding the issue at hand. One woman recalled the following experience with her mother:

My mother often suffered from severe headaches when I was a teenager living at home. Sometimes I doubted the severity of them and would say to her, "Oh, Mom, it's not so bad. Just get up and do something and you'll feel better." When I said that, she would lie down, moan, and act as if the headache had just become worse.

One day I tried a different approach and said, "Oh, I'm really sorry this goes on day after day. That must be miserable for you." To my surprise she replied, "Oh, it's not *that* bad. I'll bet it'll be gone soon. I just took an aspirin."

That's when I realized that she didn't want me to try to talk her out of her headache or even get rid of it. She just wanted me to know how she was feeling and to care about her.

This same type of validation was used by another woman whose mother was gradually losing her eyesight and complained about it continually. She reported:

I used to try to change her attitude by giving her a good dose of my positive attitude. I would say, "But Mother, think of all you *do* have. Your hearing is still good and you're basically healthy and can do so many things." It didn't work. She would complain more and say, "You just don't understand how hard this is."

Then I learned about validation. The next time she complained about her loss of vision I said, "I'll bet that's difficult, Mother." I put myself in her shoes and went on, "I think if I were losing my eyesight, I would be very frustrated, too." And in all honesty I would be.

Then the magic happened. She switched and said, "Well, it's not too bad. I can still see some and I *do* have my hearing . . . and my health is pretty good. I think I'll be grateful for that." I could hardly believe what I was hearing. That's when it seemed like the right time for a PMA, so I said, "I think you're right . . . we can be grateful for the good things."

Since I started using this approach, she complains less. I think she just kept at it before trying to get me to the point where I understood what she was going through. When I finally did, the need to complain was no longer there.

> *When validation is used, the need to complain will likely diminish or even disappear.*

That's what validation does. It allows people to come up with their own good solution and attitude. Again we see how the universal need—*I am of worth, my feelings matter, and someone really cares about me*—applies to everyone. Until we recognize and act upon this truth, a parent may keep complaining about something with the hope that we will eventually understand what she is feeling. When validation is used, the need to complain will likely diminish or even disappear.

This fact was dramatically illustrated in the following incident reported by a woman who had attended our seminar on validation. Her mother and father-in-law are in their eighties, still living independently in their own home. Her father-in-law is nearly blind, which requires his wife to do many of the chores he used to do in the past, though he still does many things quite well. He is very independent and is not one to praise, thank, or show affection. For years his wife has been highly critical of him to their children and their spouses when he was not present. The daughter-in-law reported the following:

> I stopped by one afternoon to check on them. Dad was outside working in the garden, as he loves to do, and Mom had a mountain of complaints built up inside that she could hardly wait to let erupt all over me. She began by saying, "Will you please just sit down and listen to me. No one ever allows me to say what's on my mind." That was true. Whenever she began to verbally lambast Dad we would all jump to his defense and say how hard it would be to go blind, and then we would tell her what she "ought" to do. After learning the four rules of validation —LISTEN, LISTEN, LISTEN, and UNDERSTAND—I decided to try it and to not give her any advice, as I so often did.

> She began by saying, "Dad and I can't ever talk to each other. He needs my help because his eyesight is almost gone, but he's so stubborn and independent he won't let me

help him much . . . and he gives me no affection at all."

I used a good validating phrase and said, "Hmmm. That would really be hard." And I meant it. It would be hard. She went on expressing feelings she had bottled up for a long time, saying things like, "You can't imagine how hard it is to go on day in and day out without any affection, no arm around me, no willingness to let me help, no words of appreciation when I do?" The tears were starting to flow.

I began to have compassion for her that I had never felt before and said, "Mom, that would be miserable. I'm so sorry it's happening." She continued on for a good thirty minutes or more and I stayed with her just listening and letting her go as deep as she needed to go. I only responded with, "Oh," or "Hmmm."

Then something happened. She said, "You know, it's not all Dad's fault. I have to remember he's blind, the poor dear. It must be hard to be blind." I could hardly believe what I was hearing. I had never heard her speak about him like that before. I said, "That's very kind of you to say, Mom." She looked slightly indignant and said, "Well, wouldn't you be frustrated if you went blind? Put yourself in his place." I loved it. It's like she spilled her guts on everything she needed to and then turned around and defended him.

Our conversation ended with me saying, "It sounds like you love him, Mom." She replied, "I really do and will forever." I expressed my love for her, left, and smiled all the way home.

> *Trying to change his thinking may put a stop to his progress and keep him locked into looking back more than looking forward.*

How about a father who has retired and feels lost? It works the same with him. You don't need to try to convince him that retirement can be wonderful and fulfilling. All you need do if he talks about how lonesome or even worthless he feels is to validate his feelings. He just needs a chance to express how he feels. *You don't have to make it all better.* By talking about it he will be able to come up with his own plan. Trying to change his thinking may put a stop to his progress and keep him locked into looking back more than looking forward.

If he needs help discovering new ideas for his retirement you can try some questions, such as, "What would you like to do now that you are retired, Dad?" If you have a suggestion that he might consider you could say, "Have you ever thought about . . ." When you give him your suggestion to consider you might do

well to add, "It may or may not work for you, Dad.
It's just something to consider."
That takes the pressure off and
allows him to think about it
without feeling that you will be
disappointed if he doesn't do it.
And remember, don't give him
any "you should be . . ." or
"you ought to . . ." advice. It won't work.

> *We can validate a
> parents feelings and
> still maintain our
> boundaries.*

LOVE, HONOR AND SET YOUR BOUNDARIES

Along with validating our parents there may
also be a need to set boundaries. We never need to be
swept away by someone else's needs or desires,
including those of our parents. Validation means we
walk beside them as they express their emotions, but
we are not manipulated by them. We can validate a
parent's feelings and still maintain our boundaries.
For example, let's say your mother has become a
vegetarian and enjoys this new lifestyle.   In her
enthusiasm she wants to convert everyone to her way
of thinking—especially you.   As a result she is
continually criticizing your eating habits and trying to
convince you that eating meat is tantamount to
walking through a mine field.

Since you enjoy an occasional steak and see
nothing wrong with it, you're more than a little
annoyed by her continual preaching. To put an end to

it, at least in your presence, you might try validating her feelings with a comment like, "I'm glad you enjoy the new lifestyle you've chosen, Mom, and I think it's great for you. I want you to know that I love you and appreciate your concern for me." Then follow up with your boundary, "However, I choose to eat differently. Please do not criticize my eating habits again. This is what I have decided . . . and thank you for your concern." Then change the subject and treat her normally after that. You may need to repeat this process a few times until she understands you really mean it. You may even need to drop the "please," but always speak calmly and respectfully.

Another example might be the following situation that adult children face. Your father is critical of the way you spend your money. He thinks you need to be more frugal and tells you how important it is to save your money. Every time you buy new furniture, a new car, or some other expensive item he tells you how foolish it is. He then gives a magnificent discourse on the wisdom of being more frugal and launches into stories of how he has so carefully watched his money through the years. You've heard the stories before and you don't want to hear them again. In fact, you don't want your father involved in your financial business at all. If you ask him for money, that's another matter, but we are assuming here that you didn't. What can you do?

Try validating him by saying, "Dad, I understand your concern for me. Thanks for your suggestions." You have the choice now to weigh what he has said, choose to use his ideas or not, and then leave it alone. Or you may not want anymore interference. If you don't, you can set your boundary by kindly saying, "Dad, please do not tell me how to use my money anymore. I may make some mistakes and I may not; however, I will take care of my money myself. Do not criticize my spending habits anymore." Then treat him normally after that.

A young mother reported to her mother that she didn't know how to handle a situation with her mother-in-law. Her first baby is only two months old and her mother-in-law is always giving her advice about how to take care of the baby. This new young mother is knowledgeable and capable and, though she appreciates suggestions, she resents the forceful nature of her mother-in-law's advice.

For instance, when she was taking the baby to a social gathering the mother-in-law said, "You can't take your baby there. He could get sick. You must leave him with me." The young mother was certain the baby would be fine, but didn't know how to handle the situation and felt somewhat intimidated by her mother-in-law. When asking

It's when we lose control and forget to be kind, gentle, and respectful that the relationship becomes strained or broken.

for a suggestion from her own mother, who understood the principle of validation and setting boundaries, her mother suggested that she validate her mother-in-law's feelings and concerns by saying something like, "I appreciate and understand your concerns for little Jacob," and then kindly state, "and (notice she said "and," not "but.") I would never put him in jeopardy. We are taking him with us and he will be fine."

It is important to remember that *boundaries are set by being kind, gentle, respectful, and firm.* You can set any boundary and still keep a good relationship with your parents if you stay in control of yourself and use these guidelines. It's when we lose control and forget to be kind, gentle, and respectful that the relationship becomes strained or broken. On the other hand, when we are only kind, gentle, and respectful without being firm then the problem can go on endlessly, which also leads to strained and broken relationships between parents and grown children.

This was graphically illustrated in the life of one of my clients. She was married and lived near her parents. Her mother was extremely controlling. Her actions showed that blood kin were the only important ones and treated her children's spouses more like out-laws than in-laws. She continually discounted my client's husband with comments such as, "He's lazy. He can't even get a decent job." These negative

> She treats her mother normally in every way and, at the same time, will not allow her mother to make any derogatory remarks about her husband.

feelings began to transfer to the daughter and she started treating her husband in the same manner her mother did. His deep sadness over it turned to anger and he became out of control, abusing her and their children verbally and sometimes even physically.

Because of financial difficulties he accepted a new job opportunity and they moved to another state. The mother's verbal assaults against her daughter's husband continued during every phone conversation. My client began to realize what this was doing to her and decided to come for therapy. At one point she had finally gained enough self-respect to set her boundaries with her mother. The next time her mother called and began her verbal assaults on her son-in-law, the daughter firmly and kindly said, "Do not talk about my husband like that any more."

She treats her mother normally in every way and, at the same time, will not allow her mother to make any derogatory remarks about her husband. The daughter now speaks kindly and respectfully of and to her own husband, and their relationship is significantly improved. Interestingly, her relationship with her mother is also improving.

Some parents live their lives through their children by controlling them even after they are grown and married. The control will last only as long as you allow it. The key to maintaining a good relationship after you have drawn your boundaries is to treat your parents normally. Don't withdraw by not calling or writing, or by stopping your visits with them. That behavior is not kind, gentle and respectful. *Treat them normally*. It works in perfect harmony with setting boundaries.

DEALING WITH DEATH

As our parents grow older and become ill we sometimes begin to take the opposite role and start telling them what they should do. We must remember that we are not their parents. Even if they take on some child-like qualities, they will always be the parent and we the child. They deserve our respect for that position until they draw their last breath. What they really need during these years is for us to listen to them, validate their feelings, and ask appropriate questions that will lead them to wise decisions. Sometimes that can be difficult.

When my own mother was diagnosed with terminal cancer and was told she had only a few months to live, she decided she wanted to spend those remaining months in her own home, not living with her children, and definitely not in a hospital. She was adamant. She said, "Whatever happens at the end, do what you must, but don't put me in the hospital where they will prolong my life on support systems. Promise me that." We promised. Since I was the only one of her three sons that lived near her, it became my, and my wife's, responsibility to make her wants a reality.

During the painful final months, and at her request, we learned how to give her the pain shots she needed so she wouldn't have to be hospitalized. We continued to care for her under the direction of her doctor, who said, "Just make her as comfortable as possible." My wife and I took turns staying with her. It wasn't an easy thing with a young family at home to care for. Her neighbors helped some during the late afternoon hours when our children were home from school and needed parental attention. (Now there are community programs available in most states to help in these situations. For information call your local Senior Citizens Center.)

During this time I learned the importance of validating Mother's feelings and not trying to change her thinking. I didn't always do it well at first because I really did want to solve her problems. I wanted to make everything all better and I wanted to take her pain away. I could not. Finally I realized that asking what *she* wanted and how I could help her was

> *Sometimes it is difficult to talk about death with a loved one, but mother needed to talk about it.*

the best way to handle the situation. When she would say, "It's so painful to turn over," I learned I needed to respond with, "Oh, Mother, I'm so sorry it hurts. What can I do to help?" She was the one who knew and would come up with ideas to try. Sometimes I would make a suggestion, but only a suggestion. She knew what she needed more than anyone else knew.

Sometimes it is difficult to talk about death with a loved one, but Mother needed to talk about it and we needed to listen and allow her that opportunity. I remember her saying, "I'm not afraid of death and what comes after, but I am afraid of the dying process and the pain I have to go through." All we could do was listen, validate her feelings, and be there for her. She wanted to plan her funeral and seemed to enjoy doing it. She also wanted to talk about her life experiences . . . her memories. We listened and even recorded some of these conversations. This was a choice time we shared with Mother and it not only helped her, it helped us. She also found it comforting to speak about her concept of life after death. She talked of the joy she would have meeting loved ones who had already passed on. We discovered that listening to and validating her hopes and dreams of what was to come was vitally important for her. In other conversations she told us where to find her will and other legal documents. Had she not previously prepared these items we would have needed to assist her in this process.

When her condition worsened we had to remind ourselves of our promise to her and we never, though tempted at times, said, "You need to be in the hospital where you could have professional care." She wanted to be in her familiar surroundings with family and friends. However, at one point we realized we could no longer continue what we were doing. Our five children needed us at home. That's when we had to set a boundary with mother and said, "It's time to come home and stay with us."

> *I needed to honor parental requests and yet set boundaries to preserve my own mental and physical health.*

She begged us not to take her to our home. She wanted to die where she was, in her own home, with us by her side. It was a difficult decision and we knew it was the only way we could give her the help she needed and still survive ourselves. We had no idea how much longer she would live and felt that we could serve her and our children best by bringing her to our home. A few days after we brought her home she began to slip in and out of a coma, and so we called other family members to notify them of the severity of her condition. One of my brothers was able to come and help us during that final week of her life.

This experience with my own mother taught me many things, including the need to honor parental requests and yet set boundaries to preserve my own mental and physical health, as well as my family's.

HANDLING ABUSIVE BEHAVIOR

What do you do when your parents are abusive to you? We have a friend whose elderly parents are no longer able to live alone and have moved in with her and her husband. All through her life this daughter has been verbally abused by her mother. It has been said that whatever disposition we have in our middle years will be magnified ten fold in our old age. It is proving to be true in this case. Our friend's mother is more abusive in the way she speaks to her daughter now than she has ever been. This daughter is trying to honor her parents by caring for them as a dutiful daughter "should." She says, "And it's killing me." Her mother continually says, "You're terrible and I wish I didn't have to live with you. I hate it here." Our friend said, "Then I try to convince her that I want her here and it's the best place for her and Dad to live right now. She just gets more aggressive in her abuse, often even screaming at me."

I suggested she stop trying to make her mother all better by changing her mother's feelings. Let her hate being there if she wants to. Validate her by saying, "It must be hard to leave your own home and live here." If she persists it might be well to say, "Maybe you're right, Mother. This may not be the best place for you. Where would you like to live?" She tried that approach the next day and her mother said, "We need a place of our own again, and we're going to find one." Our friend wisely said, "I understand. I have to run some errands this afternoon and while I'm out I'll look for a place for you." Her mother hasn't mentioned it since.

However, she kept abusing and insulting her daughter, but never in front of her son-in-law. She knows he won't allow it. I suggested to our friend that her mother needs to know *she* won't allow it either. A boundary needed to be set. Now when her mother starts her abusive attacks the daughter says, "You may not speak to me that way, Mother. When you're ready to be civil, then I'll talk with you." Then she walks away. Her mother is starting to treat her with more respect. She knows her daughter will not be abused any more. Our friend said, "I was about to lose my mind, but I think I'm going to be okay now. I realize that my life would have been much better if I had set boundaries a long time ago. I just didn't know I could nor did I know how."

> *No child ever needs to allow abusive treatment of any kind from parents.*

No child ever needs to allow abusive treatment of any kind from parents. Kindly setting your boundaries can dramatically improve any relationship, though in some cases it may take some time as the parent understands that the boundary is real, and so is your love for them. Some cases may need the help of a therapist. Some parents in severe cases may need medication to calm them. If you think this is needed, talk it over with your doctor.

WHEN SENILITY SETS IN

My wife's eighty-eight year old widowed mother has become quite senile. She still recognizes close family members and remembers some events, but mostly lives in a world that goes by without her even noticing. She has lost all sense of time and interest in what is happening to her or anyone else. She can no longer take care of her financial or personal affairs and has become incontinent. When her husband died nearly twelve years ago she lost all interest in living and gradually began to diminish in her mental capacity, though she is in good physical health.

When she could no longer live alone she wanted to move in with us. We, one of her sons, and another daughter shared the responsibility. Other family members would assist by taking her into their homes on weekends. After two years it became obvious to everyone that mother needed more supervised care than her children could give. We, all of her children and spouses, were agonizing over the decision to have mother live in a residential care center for the elderly. One of her sons solved the problem by planting the idea into her mind that led her to her own decision. He said, "Mother, have you ever thought about how nice it would be to live with folks your own age? You might enjoy it." She dismissed this idea at the time.

Several weeks later when she was tired of being taken nearly everywhere we went (she insisted on going and would tire and want to go home before we were ready), she said, "You all are wearing me out. I think it would be a good idea if I lived with older people." It was her decision and the family found a lovely residential care center for her. They set up a visiting schedule to insure that she would receive regular visits from family members. Such a schedule could include grandchildren, other relatives, and even old friends and neighbors.

> *It is only when loved ones fail to visit and stop giving loving attention that they feel abandoned.*

Sometimes, when it finally becomes necessary, some families must move a loved one into a care center or a nursing home who is not willing to make the move. When this happens and a parent says, "I don't want to go there. I want to stay here," the best thing anyone can do is validate their loved one's feelings with a comment like, "This must be very difficult for you, Mother." Then let her talk and freely express her feelings. Keep validating *without saying*, ". . . but you must go." I urge people to avoid the word "but" because it discounts the validating phrases. Use "and" instead when you set the boundary, such as, "I'm sad with you, Mother. I love you and want the best for you, *and* this is the right move for you." Reassure her that you will visit her often and that she will always be included in important family events. Be kind, gentle, respectful, and firm regarding the decision once it must be made. In most cases, parents make the adjustment just fine. It is only when loved ones fail to visit and stop giving loving attention that they feel abandoned.

One woman reported her need to set a boundary with her aging mother. Here's her report:

> My mother was living alone in her apartment and was able to take care of most of her personal needs. However, I became increasingly concerned about her meals. She had always enjoyed cooking and wanted to continue. I discovered that some food items were being burned while others were scarcely being warmed through. Her food preparation was unsanitary in some cases. It worried me. Sometimes she would forget to even eat. I was traveling a lot with my job and was unable to help with her meals on a regular basis. That's when I decided it was time for Meals on Wheels (a state-run program that provides meals at low cost delivered to the elderly and homebound).
>
> When I told Mother about it she was not happy. In fact, she said, "Nobody else is

going to cook my meals." I told her I understood that she had enjoyed cooking; however, now it was her time to enjoy someone else's cooking. She still resisted. I ordered the meals anyway and was with her the first day they were delivered. She looked right at the girl delivering the meal and said, "You can't make me eat that." The girl replied, "You're right, but you might like it." And she left.

The meal looked quite tasty and mother sat down and ate it while we visited. Then she said, "Tell them not to bring any more meals." I said, "Mother, the girl is going to bring you a meal every day at this same time, so I hope you will enjoy it. You've pampered everyone all your life and now it's your time to be pampered." She still was not happy about it, but the decision had been made and she went with it. Before long she became accustomed to the meals and even looked forward to them.

This woman validated her mother's feelings and then stuck to the decision that was right for her mother at that time. She kindly, gently, respectfully, and firmly set the boundary and her mother became used to it, even grew to enjoy it.

We have learned how valuable validation is with my wife's aged mother. Sometimes when we are taking her for a drive she will see a road sign to somewhere hundreds of miles away and she'll say, "Oh, let's go there." We used to reply, "That's too far away, Mom. We can't go." Then she would say, "Oh, you don't let me do anything." Now we validate her by saying, "That would really be fun." She always responds with, "Oh, let's not go. It's too far."

> *Validation is one of the finest ways we can show our parents the kindness and respect they deserve.*

Even in her failing mental capacity, whenever she is validated and allowed to express her desires and feelings she usually comes back with a logical conclusion. We find that to be quite surprising and have discovered that we don't have to talk her out of anything.

IT'S WHAT WE ALL NEED

In the end, what our parents need most, no matter their age, is what we all need—to know that *they are of worth, their feelings matter, and someone really cares about them.* Nothing feels better than to have someone love you enough to listen completely and validate your feelings. It is one of the finest ways we can show our parents the kindness and respect they deserve. We can only hope that our example will be passed on to the next generation and our children will treat us with that same measure of compassion and dignity.

BEGIN TODAY

Today is a good day to start validating your parents. Call or visit them this evening and ask, "How are you doing?" Then LISTEN by giving your full attention, LISTEN to the feelings being expressed, LISTEN to the needs, and try to UNDERSTAND. Use validating phrases such as, "I think that would be difficult. I'm sorry you're hurting." or some other appropriate phrase, and don't give any advice.

If they start telling you what to do about your life, just listen, validate and thank them for caring. You don't need to defend anything. Take what works for you and ignore the rest. If you need to restate or set a boundary, do it kindly, gently, respectfully, and firmly; then treat them normally and express your love. By practicing validation every time you visit with them it will become a natural part of your conversation. The rewards will be well worth the effort.

Chapter Twelve

How Validation Works With Divorced And Blended Families

RECOGNIZING THE MYTHS

When a divorce happens and a person wants to remarry, it is a simple thing to just start dating again, find a suitable person and get married. This marriage "should" be easier as generally the couple is a little older and more experienced. With the more maturity, the new couple "ought" to be able to get all the children to cooperate in making a "Brady Bunch" family. Right?? Wrong!!

Blending families is a challenge. When I speak of a blended family I am referring to a man and a woman, either one or both of whom have been previously married, who marry each other and either one or both have children from their previous marriage. Their children can be in the home either full-time or part-time. Those that are in the process of blending a family know the dynamics that happen and find out some of the myths the hard way. Those who have not experienced the process, either personally or through a loved one, may believe these myths. Exploring a few of the myths and the dynamics of blending may be helpful to lay the foundation for using validation.

Some of the myths are:

- Because I love you so much you will automatically love and want my children.
- Because I love you so much, my children will automatically love you and accept you as a parent.
- Your children will accept me as their parent.
- I will come in and help you raise your children in the way your other mate obviously was unable to do.
- We will be one big happy family right away.
- Now I can turn the parenting of my children over to my new mate.
- Your extended family will accept me and my children as family. They will automatically be and act as natural grandparents, uncles, aunts, etc.
- Your grown children will accept my children just like regular siblings.

- We can deal with your ex-mate with no problem.

Some of the above may turn out to be true; however, don't count on that happening right away. The process of blending a family, under the best of conditions, takes a minimum of about five years. With so many needs and problems to overcome and emotions to heal, time is a major ingredient. As much as you would like the blending to happen immediately, let it happen gradually and do not try to force it to happen. Keep in mind, you can't make things all better.

YOU ARE NEWLYWEDS

The main key to this successful blending of a family is how well the new couple puts their marriage together. Too often a remarried couple forgets they are "newlyweds." No matter their ages, this is the first time they have been married to each other. The process of discovering each other needs to be experienced anew. This is a struggle with a ready-made family. However, it must be done for the new marriage to succeed. Otherwise, you treat your new mate just like you did your "ex."

> *If a couple puts the time and energy into creating a great marriage, the children will have something stable to hold on to.*

I fully believe in the following statement: The greatest gift you can give your children is parents who love each other. This applies to marriage and remarriage. If the couple puts the time and energy into creating a great marriage, the children will have something stable to hold on to. This will hold true even if the children are in the home part-time.

When a couple marries for the first time they generally have time to adjust to each other, and to their family and friends before children arrive. In remarriage, the couple comes with a ready-made family plus an ex-mate to deal with. With divorce, there is generally much guilt, anger, frustration, sadness, and hurt. Also, there are family members and ex-in-laws who have chosen sides. If there was any abuse, neglect, or infidelity in the previous marriage, then the emotional scars are deep and slow to heal. These scars often lead to the fear that the new mate will do what was done before. Sometimes, all this emotion gets dumped on the new mate.

THE PARENTING CHALLENGE

In addition to the above, there is the dynamics of parenting. When you are there to watch the children grow up, you learn to deal with the individual characteristics of each child. The definition of what the family is developed little by little. Such things as family activities, when and how mealtimes are scheduled, chores, and money matters— allowance versus giving money when needed—all need to be redefined. The parents apply the rules of the home during the growing process. Now all of this suddenly changes and there is a strange adult to adjust to.

Also, birth order in the family, the physical home and/or room arrangements, and schools may change. Then there is a sudden shifting back and forth from one parents's home to another. All of this comes into play to turn the children's world up-side-down. To top this off, often ex-spouses are critical of the new spouse and the new rules. Sometimes they tell the children they do not have to obey the new spouse or their rules. The noncustodial parent may start a bidding war for the affection of the children using bribes and gifts to attempt to get the children to come to them.

Often, during the divorce some children become very protective of one of the parents. One friend reported his daughter and her husband moved in with him to take care of him. Another reported her son helped her with many household tasks and even helped her pay the bills.

> *A parent often runs on guilt because of all that the children are put through due to the divorce.*

They both reported that when they remarried their child was extremely hurt and felt displaced. One teenage girl told me of feeling angry toward the new husband because she no longer had the full attention and access to her mother. She said, "We used to go everywhere together. Now he has taken my mother away from me."

Another complicating aspect of blending families concerns the natural parent. This parent often runs on guilt because of all that the children are put through due to the divorce. There is an overwhelming feeling of a need to protect the children and give them special privileges. The new spouse may think, "The rules of the new home need to apply to her children but mine are different." Some noncustodial parents feel if the rules are enforced then the children will not want to come to their home. The children quickly see this and use it as a weapon to get their wants met.

DEALING WITH THE LONELINESS

There is loneliness experienced by anyone who loses a friend, a mate, or a child. Divorce, no matter how filled with anger or hurt, still brings on these feelings. With your ex-spouse you have shared hard struggles, some of the most intimate of times, possibly the birth or death of a child, and going places with each other. Now these things are gone. When a divorced person shares

> *A child needs to know it is all right to express his feelings to whichever parent he may be with.*

lonely feelings with us, we want to make it all better so he can get on with his life. Sometimes we think we need to help him feel better and we say, "You ought to be glad you don't have to put up with her anymore. Good riddance." Notice the old familiar ineffective PMA pattern. The best thing to do is to walk with the person emotionally with a few validating statements like; "I'll bet it is lonely," or "I can imagine how lonely it is." Then, just LISTEN, LISTEN, LISTEN, and UNDERSTAND.

The feeling of loneliness or of missing someone is also felt by the children. As a child attempts to understand his feelings, he may say he misses his dad. This could bring up all the hurt or anger of the divorce, resulting in a comment from the mother like, "Well, that's too bad. You will just have to get used to it." The child needs to be able to adjust and know it is all right to express his feelings to whichever parent he may be with. The statement, "It's all right to miss him" will usually allow him to put his feelings in some kind of order. His dad will always be his dad. Remember, each person needs be able to work out his own healing. Dumping any of your

> *Validating your ex may be the last thing you want to do; however, it may be the wisest choice you will make.*

unresolved feelings onto a child will not help you or the child. It will likely backfire and cause resentment toward you within the child.

COMMUNICATING WITH YOUR EX

If you are divorced and have children, generally speaking, you will have to communicate with your ex spouse regarding visits and needs of the children. In far too many cases this becomes a time of raised voices and accusations. This type of communication only magnifies the bitterness already there. If you will accept your spouse as an important person in the life of your child and treat him with the respect you yourself would like, a heavy burden of hate and anger can be lifted from your shoulders. Validating your ex may be the last thing you want to do; however, it may well be the wisest choice you will make regarding your child and your own emotional well-being.

Consider this approach when you are talking with an ex who is late with child support payments and he says, "I'm sorry. I just didn't have the money because of taxes." You could validate by saying, "Taxes are tough. I understand and I'm sorry you're having a difficult time." Then set your boundary by being kind, gentle, respectful, and firm as you say, "Nevertheless, we must have the child support payment by the 15th." If he gives further excuses, don't lose your composure and start yelling angry statements and insults. Stay calm and in control of yourself, stating your boundary. If it is possible to allow for a delay and you have found him to honor his promise to come through at a later date, do it. If he has failed in such commitments and it is necessary to state what legal action will take place, then do so kindly and respectfully, still remaining firm. Do not humiliate yourself by screaming or saying things you may later regret—things that may be repeated or heard by your child.

> *A little give-and-take for the good of the child is well worth it.*

What about your child's visits with the noncustodial parent? Unwarranted strictness regarding when your child is to return can cause unnecessary problems between the parents and the child. In one case a mother was extremely inconsiderate of the father's needs in her demands as to when the child should be brought back. It caused unnecessary anxiety in the child and caused a terrible strain on the parents' relationship and ability to negotiate on other needs of the child. I personally believe that a little give-and-take for the good of the child is well worth it. If the give-and-take is inappropriately taken advantage of, then boundaries may need to be given—always with respect.

In every case I know of, validation and the respectful setting of boundaries brings greater peace between the parents and always spills over to help create a more peaceful life for the child.

ANSWERING THE QUESTIONS

Handling questions by children, family, and

friends concerning the divorce can be a sticky problem. The questions need an adequate answer without having to give every detail. Some blended family couples I interviewed felt the best way to handle most questions was to be open, honest, and tactful. One woman stated, "When my children had questions I would answer them in an open manner that was appropriate for the age and without trying to destroy their feeling for their father. Because of this, my children seemed to have adjusted much easier and they feel free to ask me anything they would like to know."

Some children are afraid to ask the question, "Why did you get divorced?" They witnessed the pain their parents went through and they do not want to add to the pain. I have run into some children who believe *they* caused the divorce because nobody talked to them with any other information. It is astounding how often this is believed by some children of divorce. Some of my clients have carried the "my fault" feeling for many years. Most of the questions children ask can be handled with simple answers and will dispel the wrong ideas.

> If the child wants to cry and you feel like crying, cry together.

For instance, let's suppose your mate has gone off with another person. If your child asks why he or she left, you might say, "Your mom (or dad) has fallen in love with another person and has chosen to go with him (or her) and I am very sad." There is no need to go into an angry tirade when a simple answer will suffice. Again, destroying the ex-mate in the eyes of the children will not help you. Let the battles be handled in your legal negotiations with your lawyers or between the two of you—not with your child.

If the above statement is followed with a "Why" question, a simple answer could be, "I really don't know. You will have to ask your mom (or dad)." Let the child express her feelings and *validate* them with some of the validating phrases found in chapter six. If the child wants to cry and you feel like crying, cry together.

Suppose you are the one choosing to leave the marriage for a new mate. The greatest help to yourself and to others is to take responsibility for your own actions and choices. This may mean there is no definitive answer that will satisfy either your children or anyone else. To attempt to justify falling in love with someone else or having an affair by assigning fault to your mate ends up making you look foolish.

> *The child has an enormous stake in both mom and dad. They deserve a full, kind, careful, and accurate discussion.*

After all, no one forced you to make the choices you made; they are your own. Being straightforward with yourself and others is the best action to take. Simple statements like: "I know you may not understand this, but I am no longer in love with your mother and I am in love with another woman by the name of (give her name)." You can guess that the next question from the child may be, "Why?" Remember, to destroy your mate or ex-mate in the eyes of the children or anyone else will not make you look good and can hurt the children and may come back to haunt you. Stand up and take your own responsibility. Handle the questions as best you can and realize that you do not need to give all the details. Be prepared, however, to answer a lot of "Why?" questions. All must be answered gently and without guile of any kind. Since the child has an enormous stake in both mom and dad, they deserve a full, kind, careful, and honest discussion. It would help the discussion to insert one or more "That is a good question" statements here and there.

If the reason for divorce is incompatibility, then simply state, "We are not able to get along together married." Again the follow-on question may be, "Why?" Simply state the reason or reasons. The statement could be, "We have too many differences (opinions, desires, wants, goals, values, etc.), and we are not able to make them match." There are many other ways to say the same thing. Remember, trying to destroy the other person will likely cause more harm than good.

Keep in mind that, whatever you may say about the other person, whether it is good or bad, may not deter your child from loving and missing the other parent as much as he would love or miss you. If you say good things, he will likely ask "Then why did you get divorced?" Good question. Just patiently answer,

> Reinforce that the divorce was not in any way the child's fault.

letting the child take the questioning to an end that will satisfy him as much as possible. If you say bad things about your ex, the child may be deeply hurt by it. It is also possible that by so doing you might destroy some of your child's love and trust in you. Finally, there is a good chance that the questions will lead ultimately to "Why do you hate my mom (dad)?" or "Why couldn't you have hung in there for us?" or "Who's fault was it?" This may be the ultimate test of your goodness and humility. My suggestion is that you work out the answers in your mind, as much as possible, before they are asked. Such answers probably require in part a humble and sincere apology for the difficulty that the divorce has caused the child. One last question that may be in a child's mind that he may not ask is: "Was it *my* fault that you got divorced?" Be sure to reinforce that the divorce was not in any way his fault.

Finding answers for your children concerning a divorce, infidelity, or unfulfilled promises of a noncustodial parent is probably one of the hardest tasks. When children hurt or struggle, you want to make them all better. As you realize you cannot, anger may well up inside of you toward your ex-mate and it may get dumped on your children or your new mate. Validate your children's feelings and then, just LISTEN, LISTEN, LISTEN, and UNDERSTAND. If you do more, you may end up putting the children in the middle where they cannot understand and feel pushed into making a choice between the two parents.

> *Children learn the art of manipulation at a very young age because we, as parents, usually teach them.*

What about inquiring friends? Simple, straight forward answers are validating. Some people may want to probe further trying to get all the juicy details. Stay with the simple answers and you maintain your own control. At some point, your answer may need to be, "I appreciate your concern and I just do not want to go into any other details." This is an example of drawing a personal boundary while validating the interest and concern of a friend.

THE NEED FOR BOUNDARIES

I believe children have one main job in life: TO GET THEIR OWN NEEDS MET AT ALL COST. In order to accomplish this they will use whatever tools they can find. They learn the art of manipulation at a very young age. They learn it because we as parents usually teach them. They learn they can get their own way by smiling coyly, begging, whining, crying, screaming, or throwing a tantrum, particularly in public places. They also learn how to play one parent against the other. Children begin to grow up when they learn there are boundaries within which they must put their own needs and wants. They must learn to find a balance between their own needs and the needs of others. If children do not learn boundaries then they live in an unreal world of consideration for self only and, as they get older and find other people have boundaries, they get angry and become abusive.

Children who go through divorce learn they have a few more tools to use to get their own needs met. They now have three to four parents to play against each other. They recognize the guilt feelings being experienced by their parents and take full advantage of them. Then there are the step-siblings to be used as a club to gain an advantage. This sounds pessimistic and calculating; however, this is often the same as in a family in which no divorce has occurred. In divorced families the number of players and their position are different and the emotions

The more you can process the anger and hurt from the divorce the less sensitive you will be to hurtful words.

often run deeper and are in greater turmoil.

YOU ARE NOT MY DAD (MOM)

You may have heard, "You can't tell me what to do. You are not my dad (mom)!" These words echo through the corridors of the mind with great sting and hurt. This big weapon often brings out the counterattack of words from the step-parent that might result in dividing the newly married couple. The natural parent usually runs to defend her wounded child, thinking "How can anyone talk to my child like that after all he has been through?" The step-parent wanted to be accepted with all the respect and obedience due a natural parent, and it didn't happen. The battle is won by the child.

Words only have the power we allow them to have. When anyone goes through a very hurtful situation, like a divorce, words hit sensitive nerves and often trigger quick responses that ordinarily may go by the wayside. The more you can process the anger and hurt from the divorce the less sensitive you will be to such words.

To illustrate, one of my clients reported the following incident:

My wife's youngest son had a sleep-over for his eighth birthday. The next day, as the party was winding down, the living room was a mess and I wanted her son to clean up the mess and put away his toys. He did not want to do it and got mouthy. I started to raise my voice and the boy dug in his heals deeper. Finally I said, "You have five minutes to clean this room up or I will believe you do not want your toys and I will pick them up and put them away for two to three weeks. I'm setting the timer now."

The son went on complaining and didn't do it. When he realized that I was serious, he started to carry his toys upstairs to his room. I followed him up and saw his room was a disaster zone and said, "You also will have to clean up your room." With that he said, "My friends helped me make the mess so they need to help me clean it up." I ignored that statement and said, "You have to start cleaning it up by the time the timer goes off." To that the boy yelled, "You're not my dad and you can't make me do it." Then he hollered to his mother and she got involved to protect her son from what she perceived to be unfair requirements. He hadn't done it, so when the timer went off, I got a bag and gathered up the toys and put them away, all to the crying and protests of her son with his mother telling me I was being unfair.

I asked for a conference with my wife in the bathroom. Upon closing the door, I tried to explain to her what had transpired, but she had made up her mind that I had been unfair with her boy. I got frustrated, got right close to her face and yelled at her, and she slapped me. I called her names and said I didn't need this kind of marriage, and stormed out of the house. She cried and got the son's toys and gave them back to him. There is no question about it, the child won the battle and got his needs met.

[Note: When the above couple came in for therapy we talked through their individual needs regarding the above incident and how the child had effectively played one against the other to get his needs met. They realized the need to build a strong marriage and to work out the differences in their parenting styles. They discussed the ways they could help meet each other's needs and committed to work hard at fulfilling that commitment. They are now experiencing success by working together better.]

Sometimes it is hard for the children to know what to call the new husband or wife.

So how do you handle the statement "You're not my father (mother)?" Often there is confusion on the part of both the children and the parents concerning the correct title for a step-parent. I would suggest the couple meet with each set of children for the purpose of approaching this subject. This would be ideal just before the marriage and if it is after, do it now. During this meeting, the step-parent could say something like, "I want you to know that I recognize I am not your father. You have a father and he will always be your father. I am your mother's husband and I love her very much and will support her, and I want very much to be your friend. Sometimes it is hard to know what to call the new husband. I want you to be comfortable so if you want to call me 'dad' or by my first name, either one will be fine with me." This, or some dialogue like this, may take some of the craziness out of the situation of blending a family.

I had a couple, in my office, accompanied by her two young boys, ages five and seven. There was a power struggle going on as the parents were insisting on the title "Dad" and the two young boys were not happy with this and seemed to be confused. So I scripted the step-father through a dialogue much like the above. I even asked the boys if the step-father was their father and their answer was, "No." When the boys were given the choice they both chose to call him "Dad."

Their countenance seemed to indicate they were relieved to see they had a choice and that the new husband recognized their natural father. That is validation. The step-father listened to the boys and understood their needs. The following week, the parents reported hearing a conversation between the boys that followed an argument. One of the boys said, "I'm going to tell Dad on you!" The other one said, "That's OK 'cause he's my friend."

> *If the children sense the parents are divided on the rules, they will skillfully play one parent against the other.*

Even after this type of dialogue, a child may still throw the phrase, "You're not my dad." *Validate* that statement by saying, "You are right, I'm not your dad. However, I am your mother's husband and I support her rules." The child may say, "I don't like that rule." Validate the statement by saying, "That's all right to not like the rule and we can discuss it when your mom gets home." Then *kindly, gently, respectfully,* and *firmly* state, "Until then, the rule will be followed."

SETTING THE RULES IN A BLENDED FAMILY

Rules in any family can be set only when both parents agree to the rules and that they must apply to all the children and for the most part the adults also. If the children sense the parents are divided on the rules instead of united, they will then use that as a weapon to get their own needs met by skillfully playing one parent against the other. In the example above, the son knew if he got the step-father angry enough his mother would come rescue him. He had found out they were not united on rules and he could get by the rules by whining and pestering his mother enough until he had worn her down into submission.

This kind of struggle occurs in all families to some extent. When the boys of a separated couple were asked what their part in the family discord was, they each said they knew if they got Dad mad enough their mother would come to their rescue and argue with their dad. The end result would be they might get out of doing what their dad asked. The separation was not the children's fault. The parents needed to stop their manipulation by unitedly maintaining the family rules.

In setting rules it is important to first have the couple meet together and decide on the basic rules they both can support, then meet with each set of children separately. During this meeting, the natural parent needs to take the lead. Discuss the new needs of the blended family and get suggestions on rules and procedures from the children with the step-parent participating. After the rules and procedures are set, the step-parent voices his support to the natural parent and the rules. If during the discussion or after, one of the children states, "We didn't used to have to have all these rules. I don't like it." Validate the statement by saying, "You are right and I understand you don't like it. It was a struggle when our family changed and the rules needed to change." Do not say any more than that because further explanation just muddies the discussion. You do not have to make it all better; just understand the child's point of view.

This rule-setting procedure is one I would suggest for all families. The parents must agree on the philosophy of how their home is to be run and the rules that apply to all. Then get the children's input. The next step is to have both parents voice their support for the rules and expectations, and to voice their support for each other. Even after getting all this done, some children will fight the rules because they want to get their needs met. If this occurs, listen to the child and then say, "Nevertheless, the rules must be kept." Then follow through, being *kind, gentle, respectful,* and *firm.*

One couple had a unique experience with the need for equal treatment. The wife hollered to her own children to tell them to accomplish some task. It was not done disrespectfully; it was just loud calling from one room to another or from one floor of the house to another. Her children were used to this. She stated she could not do this to his children because she did not know how they were brought up and she was afraid it would offend them. Both sets of children were teens and above in age.

One day a couple of his children said to her, "Do you really care about us? You yell at your own kids and if you don't yell at us, we don't think you love us." I am not advocating yelling; however, this incident seems to point out that sometimes unequal treatment may be interpreted as unequal love.

How do you handle the statement of a child who says to the other parent, "My mom (dad) says I don't have to obey your rules." The child could also say he did not have to obey the step-parent. This could key in a return of the anger or hurt you experienced before or during the divorce and may be turned on the child. Also, there is

> *Threatening to never come again can become the ultimate weapon used to manipulate the noncustodial parent.*

another thought. The child may report a statement that may not have been made by the other parent. Whoever said, "Children never lie" never had children. Not all children lie; most just stretch the truth so they can get their needs met. So how do you validate the statement, "My mom says I don't have to obey your rules?" Try this, "Son, I hear what you are saying. However, your mother has rules in her home and I expect you to obey those. We have rules in our home and I expect you to obey them, even if they are different." To that he might say, "Then I won't come to visit you anymore!"

Threatening to never come again can become

the ultimate weapon used to manipulate the noncustodial parent. I have known some men (as men are usually the noncustodial parent) who fear this and they give in to the child. Once you have given in to this threat, it will be used over and over again. It is important that boundaries are drawn, always remembering they are *kind, gentle, respectful,* and *firm.* To his comment you may say, "That would make me very sad and would not be my choice. I will continue to invite you to come because I love you, and I realize you have a choice to come or not. I hope you will come. We will always attempt to be fair and there will always be rules to follow." The child may choose not to come for a period of time. Continue to invite without trying to bribe with things or trips unless the things and trips are in your normal routine or plans.

> *If you place yourself in competition you then set yourself up to be manipulated.*

The more energy you use to create a good marriage and as normal a home life as possible, the more appealing your home will be to your children. Your home will then be a safe place and a pleasant place to be. If both the custodial and noncustodial parents create such homes, the safer and better adjusted the children will be. This may sound unrealistic but it is not. Remember, the only person you can control is yourself and the only home you can work on is yours. You don't need to worry about any one else's as you are not in competition. If you place yourself in competition you then set yourself up to be manipulated.

UNFULFILLED PROMISES

Sometimes parents make statements or promises that are not kept or fulfilled. Unfulfilled promises are hurtful to anyone and after a divorce they produce even more emotions. The custodial parent is acutely aware of the child's emotional needs and is very protective. This, too, could be a time when the anger and disappointment of the divorce comes to the surface. This is not the time or place to process it as it will harm the child more than help. If the child asks, "Why hasn't (doesn't, can't,) daddy come to see me?" or "Why doesn't daddy send me a birthday present?" or "Why didn't mommy come pick me up?" The first answer could be, "I don't know." Then the child may express her anger, frustration, or sadness. Validate her feeling by saying something like, "I think I understand how you feel. I would be (whatever the expressed emotion was) also." Then, if the child says, "Well why didn't he come?" The answer needs to refer the child back to the source by saying something like. "I don't know. I guess you will have to ask your dad when you see him next." Talking down the other parent will not do any good for anyone.

THE MORE PEOPLE WHO LOVE

My wife has often said, "The more people who love and care about your children the better off they are." Children prosper in a loving and respectful environment. If the parents of divorced children and their extended families would remember this, they would help decrease the victimization of their children. Grandparents can play an important role if they will let themselves. The problem is they are parents also and run to protect their own children. After the divorce, if the grandparents want to be involved with the grandchildren, they must find a way to be accepting of the ex-mate.

Sometimes the grandparents dump their own unresolved emotions onto the grandchild. If the grandparents have developed a trusting relationship with the grandchildren, the grandchildren will feel safe asking them questions they find hard to ask their parents. An example of this was reported by one grandmother of a five-year-old boy in the following scenario:

About three years after our son's divorce, his little boy (who lives with his mother) and I were looking through one of my memory books of family photographs and memorabilia. He had brought the book to me and wanted to go through it and talk about what was in it. The book was open on the floor as we looked through it. To my surprise he turned a page and there was a picture of his mother and father on their wedding day. (I had forgotten it was in this particular book.) He looked at it and said, "That's my mom and dad, isn't it, Grandma?" I said, "Yes. That's when they got married." Then he looked right at me and said, "Why did they get a divorce?"

That's when I realized he needed to talk about it with me and I had to be someone he could count on for straight answers. It was a difficult spot to be in. I took a deep breath and answered as honestly and nonjudgmentally as I could by saying, "Mommy did not want to live with Daddy anymore and decided to move out and get a divorce."

He stood up, stomped his foot on his mother's picture and cried, "Stupid dummy Mommie!" I listened as he poured out his anger at his mother, then hugged him, and said, "Things happen that we don't always understand." He calmed down and I said, "The good thing about it all is that you have a good mother who loves you very much and you have a good daddy who loves you very much, too. And I love you very much." He relaxed and turned the page.

I knew I could not blame his mother, even though inside I did not approve of her actions. That's not my place. My place is to build a loving relationship with my grandson and I knew I could only do that if I wasn't critical of either parent.

> Grandparents can play an important role in the lives of grandchildren when they create the atmosphere that allows the child to talk openly and freely.

This grandmother provided a safe place for her grandson to be able to express his feelings. Not taking sides with either parent allowed the boy to know he could say what he needs to say in the future without his grandmother putting his mother down or blaming her.

My wife had an experience with our six-year-old grandson—who is also a child of divorce—one afternoon when she took him out for pizza. They were sitting at the table waiting for the order to come when, out of the blue, our grandson said, "Grandma, divorce stinks!" She validated his feelings by saying, "I'm with you. I think it stinks, too." He said, "Yeah, it does." Then he went back to his conversation about school. It seemed he just needed to say it to someone who understood and wouldn't give him a "nice" little speech about it.

Grandparents can play an important role in the lives of grandchildren when they create the atmosphere that allows the child to talk openly and freely. There is no need to dump the hurt or judgmental attitude on the children of divorce. When the children are free to talk they can process what they need to process and some of the wounds of the divorce can begin to heal. In the following poem my wife tenderly expressed the inner thoughts of a child torn apart by divorce and the gentle healing that a grandparent can bring.

Child of Divorce

My mom and dad went separate ways,
And it's hard to understand.
I love them more than words can say . . .
It's not at all the way I planned.

I cry about it in the night
And wish for yesterday,
Then pray for sleep so happy dreams
Will chase my tears away.

Why did it have to happen?
Did I commit some awful sin?
If I change myself somehow
Will they fall in love again?

I asked these many questions
To my grandma just last week.
Her loving arms held me close
As I heard her gently speak:

"My child, it's not because of you.
You didn't make the slightest scar.
And you don't need to change one bit,
You're wonderful the way you are.

We may never really know
What caused the break we mourn.
But the best thing that ever happened
Was that you were born.

Oh, please believe me, dear one,
For the words I speak are true,
They may not love each other,
But they always will love you."

— Joy Saunders Lundberg

BEGIN TODAY

Begin today by going back through this chapter and picking out one idea that you think could work in your family. Discuss it with your spouse and decide on the way the two of you can implement it. Remember the importance of validating each other and your children. It takes practice but will pay big dividends.

Chapter Thirteen

———•••••———

How Validation Works With Friends

WHAT IS A FRIEND?

Before discussing how validation works with friends, it might be well to define what a friend is. When asking clients and those attending our seminars what they consider a true friend to be, the following five attributes are always mentioned: (1) someone I can trust, (2) someone who accepts me as I am and won't judge me, (3) someone I can have fun with, (4) someone I can talk to, (5) someone who really cares about me and is there for me. These statements combine to make an excellent definition.

A few years ago my wife wrote the following poem that embodies some of the important qualities of true friendship.

My Friend

Who reaches out to me
And understands
With unconditional love
And no demands?
Who listens to my plea
And feels my pain?
Who makes this crazy world
Of ours seem sane?

Who shares the deepest joys
I sometimes feel?
Who is it I can trust
And know is real?
Who brings to cloudy days
A welcome light?
Who smiles and helps a wrong
Turn into right?

Who walks with faith and hope
Along life's path?
Who turns to God
And pleads in my behalf?
Who loves and cares no matter
Where or when?
The answer is so clear—
It's you,
My friend.

— Joy Saunders Lundberg

WE ALL NEED A FRIEND

There is nothing quite so wonderful as having someone to share in your happiness. When you get that long-hoped-for promotion, when you return from a fun trip and want to share the details with someone, or when a child does something that makes you proud, isn't it fun to tell it to a friend who listens and rejoices with you? It somehow magnifies the joy.

A friend of ours, who feared she had cancer and was waiting for the results of the tests, called my wife and me one day and said, "It's negative! They found the problem and it isn't cancer!" She was thrilled and so were we. She knew we cared about her and would be with her either way. It was a

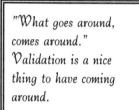

"What goes around, comes around." Validation is a nice thing to have coming around.

beautiful and sweet moment to be able to share in her happiness and relief. Letting friends share their feelings of joy and walking with them in that joy is a deeply rewarding form of validation.

On the other hand there is also nothing quite as important as having a good friend to tell your troubles to. One woman said, "I have heard my friend talk about her divorce again and again, expressing her anger and heartache over all that happened. I decided she needed to have someone she could do this with who would listen no matter how many times she said it and would not try to talk her out of any of those feelings. My experience tells me that at some point she'll realize she is sick of talking about it and that's when she'll be through with it and ready to move on."

What a great gift this woman is giving to her friend. And she is right. At some point her friend will put it all aside and move on with her life and into new conversations, and with this kind of validation it will happen for her much sooner than it would without it. A nice side to this is that in the process she will learn from her friend's example how important validation is and will be able to give it back to her whenever she may need it for difficult situations she may face—and we all face them. There is a popular saying, "What goes around, comes around," and I believe it. Validation is a nice thing to have coming around.

DON'T TELL A FRIEND WHAT TO DO

Compare the situation of the woman mentioned above with the experience I described in the introduction of this book which was:

I had had an extremely hard day at the office. Nothing seemed to go right. I sat down with my close friend and wanted to just tell him what I had experienced. As I started to tell him he would break in with what he thought I could have done or what I could now do to solve my problem. I didn't need this kind of help. Inside I felt like screaming, "Be quiet and listen to me. I need to tell someone what went on before I burst and I thought you really cared about me and would understand." I felt frustrated, ended the conversation quickly, and left feeling sad and hurt.

The contrast is significant. Had my friend listened and validated my feelings instead of breaking in with solutions to my problem, I would have left with a completely different feeling.

There is nothing quite so demeaning and unfulfilling as having a friend tell you what you "should" do or "ought" to do about the things you are experiencing. True friendship means you listen without giving advice. You may be thinking, "But what if I have a great idea that would help her?" I say, keep it to yourself for a time. Remember the four rules of validation: LISTEN by giving your full attention, LISTEN to the feelings being expressed, LISTEN to the needs, and try to UNDERSTAND. If you are thinking of solutions to her problems while she is sharing her feelings and thoughts with you, then you are not giving her your full attention.

My wife experienced the need for this when she was in a deep conversation with one of her friends.

Here's her experience:

> My friend was pouring her frustrations out to me regarding a conflict she was having with a family member. It was an extremely difficult problem for her and as she spoke she started to cry. I was validating her feelings as she talked and cried, and it wasn't hard to do because my heart was with her. I sincerely felt sorrow over what she was going through and said, "I'm so sorry this is happening to you." And then my tears started coming. I said, "I can't stand that this is happening to you. I really care about you." She smiled a little smile through her tears and said, "Thank you so much. That means everything to me right now."
>
> Then I fell into that trap of thinking I had a solution for her and said, "I've got an idea you might try." Then I gave her my idea. As soon as I switched into that problem-solving mode her tears stopped and her expression changed. She said, "That won't work. I've already tried it. Well, I've got to go now."

If you are a true friend you will allow him to freely express his feelings, let him go to the depth he needs to go without standing in his way by trying to change his thinking or by trying to talk him out of his feelings.

I couldn't believe I had done it. I had not allowed her to go down as far as she needed to go with her emotions. I stood in her way with what I thought was a good solution for her. This experience reinforced in my mind the importance of not giving a solution. I needed to just validate and listen. I could have called or visited her another time and asked a few questions that might have led to her own solutions and even given a suggestion then, but not in the heat of that moment when she was pouring out her deepest feelings to me.

We all need to free ourselves from this unnecessary problem-solving obligation by keeping this phrase in mind: I DO NOT HAVE THE POWER TO MAKE MY FRIEND ALL BETTER. The solutions to her problems lie within herself. If you are a true friend you will allow her to freely express her feelings, let her go to the depth she needs to go without standing in her way by trying to change her thinking or by trying to talk her out of her feelings. Let her have those feelings and you will be surprised at how she will pull herself back up. When people are given that opportunity they usually come up with their own answers. Talking it out gives them the chance to gain a new perspective.

SETTING BOUNDARIES WITH FRIENDS

One woman said, "I have a friend who drives me nuts. When it comes to disciplining my children she's always telling me what I should have done or what I ought to do next time. I get so tired of it that I don't really want to be with her any more." She expressed her sadness over this because she said there were things about her friend she enjoyed, but it just wasn't worth the friendship to have to suffer through her lectures. She said, "She always makes me feel foolish and stupid because I don't know as much as she does. And I just don't need that."

So what can be done in this situation? I suggest that a few boundaries need to be set. Remembering that boundaries are set by being *kind, gentle, respectful,* and *firm,* she could say to her friend, "Please stop telling me how to discipline my children unless I ask you for a suggestion. It's putting a strain on our friendship and there are so many things I *do* enjoy about our friendship that I don't want to lose it." If she does not respond favorably to this boundary, then you can assume it was not a genuine friendship after all. Generally speaking, a good friend will apologize and not violate the boundary.

Now let's say you are the friend who usually gives the advice. How do you handle the situation? Suppose your friend's toddler just unstrung her favorite music cassette tape while the two of you were visiting. As soon as she realizes what he has done she grabs him by the arm, spanks him and yells, "Don't you ever do that again!" The child bursts into tears and screams as she hauls him off to his room. You sit there thinking of a much better way to handle the situation and are itching to "teach" her what she "should" have done. Don't do it! Stop right now and think what she really needs. Isn't it a little validation? After all, her favorite tape has just been ruined.

When she comes back into the room she'll likely say, "I don't know what I'm going to do with that child. He's always destroying something . . . and now it's my favorite tape." This is the time to validate her feelings by saying something like, "It's frustrating when kids do things like that." If you're honest you will agree that times like this *are* frustrating. Then let her talk. She'll likely tell you other things he has done that frustrated her. She needs to be able to unload these frustrations on someone who cares enough to just listen without trying to teach her anything. THIS IS NOT THE TIME TO TEACH. IT IS THE TIME TO LISTEN.

At some point she may say, "What would you do if you were me?" The best thing you can say to that question is, "I'm not sure. What else have you tried?" or "What else could you do?" Let her try to come up with some better solutions of her own. This is her problem, not yours. Just talking about it will help her get a better perspective. After she has explored her own thinking and still doesn't know what to do, you might give a suggestion by saying, "I don't know if this will work with your child—they're all so different—but here's a suggestion you might try." (Notice the no-pressure approach.) Then give your suggestion and maybe even add, "You'll probably think of something better, but this might be worth a try. It's not easy raising kids."

That's a validating friendship. That's the kind of friend you will likely choose to spend your time with. No one is belittled and no one appears to have all the right answers. Remember, what works for you and your child may not work for her. She has to make her own discoveries. If, at a later date, you find a magazine article or a book with some good ideas that helped you, you may want to share it with her. No strings attached—just some ideas to consider.

What about a friend who starts monopolizing your time? This can become a serious problem and even ruin the friendship. I observed this with a client I'll call Joan, who had been friends with another woman, a widow, for several years.

My client had other friends, too, and yet she especially valued her friendship with this particular friend. However, this friend felt the need to be with my client an inordinate amount of time and the friendship became suffocating. My client had to set a boundary for her own survival and let her friend know what schedule worked for her. She said, "I value our friendship and I need to talk to you about some of my needs." Notice how she didn't say "but I need to talk to you . . ." Had she used the word "but" it could have been taken to discount the friendship. When her friend realized she would not be seeing Joan as often she said, "I enjoy our friendship, too, and I'll miss not seeing you more often." My client validated that feeling by saying, "I understand. We've had some great times together and I want that to continue. How about if we get together every Saturday?" Her friend agreed and they have been spending nearly every Saturday afternoon together. They both adjusted and seemed happy with the arrangement.

I believe a true friend will honor your boundaries and be understanding. How about a friend who keeps pressing you for details of your life you don't wish to talk about? You can set a boundary by validating her feeling with, "I appreciate your interest; however, I don't wish to talk about that." Then change the subject and move on, treating her normally.

What about a friend who presses you to do something against your own personal value system? Once again, set your boundary. You know what you believe and how far you will go in certain situations. In a *kind, gentle, respectful,* and *firm* way, SET YOUR BOUNDARY. If you are wishy-washy about it, there is no boundary. If you are

> *A true friend accepts you the way you are and will not judge you.*

not sure of your own values I strongly suggest you spend some time alone and seriously contemplate, even write down, your own personal values. To have them firmly in your own mind will be a great help to you and may keep you from making mistakes you will later regret.

Remember, a true friend accepts you the way you are and will not judge you. If that isn't happening in a friendship then I believe it is not a true friendship. A true friend will accept and honor your boundaries.

WHEN A FRIEND LOSES A LOVED ONE

One woman reported the following experience she had in validating a friend whose husband had recently died of a heart attack:

When it first happened I was devastated. I could hardly bear to have my friend go through such a difficult experience. I wanted to make everything all better for her, but that was not possible. When we were together I put my arms around her and said, "I am so sorry." We held on to each other and sobbed together for several minutes. Then she said, "It all happened so quickly and now he's gone." I did not try to cheer her up. That's absurd to even think I would try at a time like this. I said, "What happened?" She seemed to want to tell me every detail and I just stayed with her and listened.

At some point she said, "I don't know what I'm going to do." I believe at that moment, if I had not learned about validation, I would have given her some advice as to what she "should" do. Thank goodness I didn't. That was not what she needed. All I said to that comment was, "I'm sure it will be difficult. Is there anything you would like me to do that would help you?" Her concern seemed to be with the funeral arrangements and she asked for my help regarding those needs. When she said, "I don't know what I'm going to do," I thought she was talking about her future and would have given her advice regarding that, not the funeral. I saw how important it was for me to ask her what she needed, not assume what she needed.

My wife had an experience with a new neighbor whose grandmother died. She did not know the neighbor well, but wanted to express her condolences. Our neighbor invited her in and my wife said, "I'm sorry to hear about your grandmother's passing." The neighbor expressed her appreciation for her concern. Then my wife said, "Tell me about your grandmother." She spent the next thirty minutes talking about the many wonderful times she and her grandmother had enjoyed together. She cried and she laughed at some of the memories. My wife hugged her and said, "Thanks for sharing with me. I can see why you would love her so much." That was the beginning of a sweet friendship with our neighbor. At the time of a death nothing heals as magically as does the listening ear of a friend. That's validation.

A friend of mine shared the following experience he had that further illustrates the power of validation.

A few years after my wife died, my two teenage boys got involved with drugs and were creating some problems in the neighborhood. It was an extremely difficult time for me. I missed my wife terribly and seemed to have lost control of my boys. It was a time of great sorrow for me. One neighbor, who happened to be a lawyer, was so outraged by my boys' behavior that he threatened to have them taken away from me. I felt abandoned.

The following week I attended a social gathering nearby and felt very lonely because no one spoke to me. As I was walking away, about to get into my car and leave, a man from my neighborhood came up to me, put his arm around my shoulders and said, "It's kinda rough, isn't it?" All of a sudden I felt like somebody understood and really cared about me. It was a turning point for me, and though it happened fifteen years ago, I still remember it as though it happened yesterday.

The power of one friend validating your feelings and walking with you in your emotions is inestimable.

LET THEM ENJOY A MINI CATHARSIS

Sometimes in validating a friend, you can allow her the relieving and almost purifying effects of a mini catharsis. For example, perhaps your friend is upset at something her ex-husband said to her and she says to you, "I'm so furious at him I'd like to punch his lights out." Rather than responding with, "Oh no—you can't do that. That would only make matters worse," like so many of us do, how about enjoying her catharsis with her by saying, "Yeah, I think I might feel that way, too!" She might say, "Oh, wow, that would be so great!" Watch her smile as she imagines the scene. You will see the tension release and then she will likely say, "Oh well, I couldn't really do that. It's just that he makes me so mad sometimes." Then just validate her feelings with, "That's got to be difficult," and allow her to talk it out. She'll come around to some good solutions that work for her if she is given the opportunity to express her feelings without you standing in her way emotionally.

BEGIN TODAY

Sometime during the day or this evening call a friend and ask her (or him), "How are you doing?" If her response is, "I'm fine. How are you doing?" Briefly respond and ask, "What's going on in your life?" She may say, "Why?" You could say, "I haven't talked to you in a while and I'm just interested in what's going on with you." Then listen and validate her feelings without giving any advice. If she asks you for help or solutions, refer to chapter six and use some of the validating phrases and questions to help her reach inside herself for her own best solutions.

Begin today to discover the joy of a friendship that allows you to just listen and understand, and does not require you to be responsible for solving your friend's problems.

Chapter Fourteen

How Validation Works On The Job

CUSTOMER RELATIONS

At one time I was a co-owner of a small electronics business. Customer relations and employee relations occupied a great deal of my time. Responding to the needs of both was an important and often difficult task. I wanted my employees to take a real interest in their work and to believe they were an integral part of all we were doing. It was important for them to know that when they answered the phone they were the personification of everyone and everything we did there at the business. Each supervisor needed to know they were the representatives of management and what we stood for.

> *All we had to offer over any other company was the service and caring we gave.*

In the end, all we had to offer over any other company was the service and caring we gave. I believe every business owner wants to engender within each employee the feeling in the statement that I have heard for years: The customer is number one. If we don't take care of our customers, somebody else will.

In the introduction of this book I gave the example of a customer service representative on the phone with an irate customer. To the customer on the other end of the phone that representative is the company all rolled up in one person. Here is the example again:

The phone on my desk rang and I answered it. In a very loud irritated voice the man said, "I hope you can help me because I have now talked to three other people and I want something done! My car has been in your lousy shop three times in the last two weeks for the same problem and it still isn't fixed!" I said, "Could you tell me what is wrong with it now?" and he replied "If I knew what was wrong with the #@*#@ car I would have fixed it myself." I responded with, "I'm sorry you are having such trouble." He broke in and said, "I'll say you're sorry. You are the sorriest bunch of people I know. Now what the @#$#@ are you going to do to fix my car?" I found myself responding angrily, "Hey look mister, it's not my fault your car isn't fixed!"

Let's see if there is a better way to handle the situation. We will stop the example right after the customer's statement, "Now what the @#$#@ are you going to do to fix my car?" What is the emotional state of the customer? Have you ever been in a similar situation where it appears nobody seems to care about your problem? What did you want to happen? How did you want to be responded to? Remember, validation is walking with another person emotionally from where they are to where they need to go.

I think the customer above is feeling a mixture of emotions: *Mad* because the car is not fixed, he has not had use of his car for at least three days in the last two weeks, and nobody seems to care; *Sad* because the car is not fixed, he believes he is alone in his problem, and years ago before they computerized cars he used to be able to fix some things on his car; *Afraid* because maybe his car can't be fixed, maybe he will have to get another car and he likes this one, and maybe there isn't anyone who really cares about his problem. These emotions generate frustration and the need to dump the frustration somewhere.

When a customer dumps the frustration on you, you need to understand that this has nothing to do with you personally, though it seems directed at you. Step back and listen with that part of you that has had similar feelings. Maybe, when this is done, your response could be something like: "That's got to be frustrating. Apparently we have let you down and I'm sorry. There's no excuse for this, and I am going to take personal action to make sure we meet our responsibility. When can we have your car back?" *This is validation.* It shows you understand his frustration. Then say, "While your car is here and you have any question, please call me. I will personally find out what is happening. Thank you for your patience." All people need to know that *they are of worth, their feelings really matter, and someone cares.*

For example, I had a problem with a rebuilt toner cartridge for my copier. When I went back to the first company to tell them the cartridge wasn't working properly, the treatment I received from the owner was as if he were saying, "How dare you question our product. We do outstanding work and it obviously is something you are doing wrong."

I went to another company and bought another rebuilt cartridge. It, too, had a similar problem and the response was completely different. I called them and the owner said he would bring out another cartridge, which he did. It, too, had a problem. He said, "Let me pick up your copier and test these cartridges until we find one that will work in your machine. This will be at no additional cost to you." He did just that. I now have a cartridge that works, I have bought another cartridge from him for my printer, and I will tell other people about the wonderful service I received from that company. This man cared about my problem, listened to my need, understood, and offered his help. That's validation!

NOT ALL NEEDS CAN BE MET

There may be times when requests are made that are not possible to meet. Suppose the customer with the car problem demands you take back the car and give him all his money back. How do you validate a request like that? This is the time you must know your limits and can comfortably state them. For instance, you might say, "That would be nice and I wish I could but I am not able to do that. However, I will work very hard to see that your car is fixed to your satisfaction." His response could still be a frustrated comment such as, "Then I will go to your competitor. I'm sure he will welcome my business." Validate by saying, "I think I can understand how you feel. I apologize for not being able to do what you ask. I will feel sad to lose your business. I would like the opportunity to fix your car correctly and will understand if you choose to go elsewhere."

Not all problems have a solution to meet everyone's needs. If you maintain your own control, in a way similar to the above, you have the best chance to get his business back. You will also maintain your reputation for treating customers kindly.

There are limitations to all that we do. Being able to work comfortably within those boundaries is the challenge. To wish the boundaries were not there and to even state your desire to have them gone is all right. This can be validating to the person you are talking with. You show your comfort level by how you present the limits and your acceptance of them. I have wished to have some rules changed only to find out they could not be changed. My feelings about the business were good when the person I talked to understood my desire, validated my need, and kindly told me "No" or "It isn't possible."

CARING IS THE KEY

A statement quoted previously says, "I don't care how much you know until I know how much you care." This idea is born out in an article that appeared in a Guidepost Magazine[18] several years ago. It told the following story of a nurse who went to work in a government convalescent home:

> She'd been assigned to an elderly patient who had not spoken a single word in three years. The other nurses disliked this patient so much that she always was passed down to the newest member of the staff. But this nurse was a Christian, at least she'd always thought she was and she decided that her Christian love was only as good as her

love for this particular patient.

The old woman used to sit in a rocking chair all day long. "So I pulled up another rocking chair," the nurse said, "and just rocked alongside her and loved her and loved her and loved her." The third day she opened her eyes and said "You're so kind." Those were the first words she had spoken in three years.

> *Validation is being with someone where they are, not where you think they ought to be.*

The article went on to say that in two weeks the elderly woman had recovered sufficiently to go home. Evidently the other nurses had labeled her as a crabby unresponsive woman and treated her as such. What does this have to do with validation? You see, validation is being with someone where they are, not where you think they *ought* to be. Too often we decide where someone *ought* to be by how we feel or by what we understand. It does not work. The only way we can help someone is to listen and try to understand where they are and where they have been. When the new nurse decided to be with the elderly woman where she was, she accepted her on her terms and didn't try to force a change. When the elderly woman felt the warmth of caring she opened her emotional door and let the nurse in. It was then the nurse could offer her help.

Caring is the key. Often while explaining a situation or need to a caring, listening person, people come up with their own solution to their own problem. All you need to do is ask a few validating questions, then LISTEN, LISTEN, LISTEN, and UNDERSTAND.

WATCH FOR EXAMPLES

It is fun to attempt to find examples of validation during television programs and movies. There was a marvelous example during one *Matlock* program (a story about a fictional lawyer in practice in Atlanta, Georgia). The prosecuting attorney and Mr. Matlock were arguing about the admissibility of some new evidence presented by Matlock in the courtroom. The judge called them to his chambers for a conference. During the discussion the prosecuting attorney said, "This is terrible. The police had plenty of time to get this evidence." Matlock replied, "Y'know, your Honor, this really is terrible. It is terrible the police took so much time." To that the prosecutor said, "Well, I guess we can work with this." The judge then left the room and the prosecutor said to Matlock, "I don't like this at all." Matlock replied, "I wouldn't like it either." With that the prosecutor relaxed and the scene faded.

This was not a real scene yet it showed one of the benefits of validation. When a person is listened to and understood, there is nothing to argue about. If Matlock had said, "That's too bad. You will just have to work with it," he would have had the beginnings of a real fight. As it was, the prosecutor had nothing to fight about. The situation he had to deal with was uncomfortable and not ideal. He stated it and was understood and validated. I have seen this type of situation happen in real life. When one person is validated by another person there is nothing to argue about.

It is helpful to observe others using or not using the principles of validation in their work. These observations can assist you in learning how or how not to do it in your own situations.

My wife, Joy, observed a situation while waiting in a line at a post office window. She overheard a conversation between the clerk and the person in front of her.

The clerk seemed out of patience and harried. At the conclusion of an involved transaction, the clerk abruptly put the change on the counter. The customer said, "I don't appreciate the way you are treating me. You threw my change at me." The clerk defended herself, saying, "I did not. I just set it there." The customer said, "You have an attitude!" and walked away disgruntled. I thought to myself, the customer would have gone away happier if the clerk had just said, "I'm sorry. I didn't mean to seem abrupt."

I stepped up to the window and the clerk was still flustered and out of sorts. My heart went out to her and I said, "Some days are really rough aren't they?" The clerk immediately softened and said, "Today has been a bad one." She was pleasant as she waited on me and seemed to have a shift in attitude.

Joy was right. The customer before her would have gone away happier had the clerk validated the customer instead of defending herself. Notice how the clerk's attitude changed when she was validated by the understanding phrase, "Some days are really rough." It works both ways—the worker or the customer, either one, can use validation and smooth things out.

THE VALIDATING TEACHER

There are some occupations where the people you deal with are not looked on as customers. For instance, a teacher does not look upon her students as customers when in all actuality they are her customers—the consumers of her product of learning. I remember while I was a youngster in school I had a desire to learn but I wanted to expend as little energy and work as possible. After all, it was more fun to play or visit with my friends than to read, study, and do homework. One approach students use to possibly get the work load reduced is to complain, and I did my share of it.

One of our neighbors teaches English at a local university. She told of how she used to handle student complaints and how she changed her approach by using validation with the students. Here's her experience:

At the beginning of the semester I would explain the plan for the class, reasons for the assignments, the number of assignments, and what the research showed to back up my requirements   As the semester got in full swing, some of my students would come to me and complain about the number of assignments, the time it took to fulfill the assignments, the strictness of having to do papers a certain way, and the number of ungraded writing assignments.   I would, again, go through the same explanation as I did at the first of the semester and it didn't seem to help.

After learning about validation, I decided to try it. When my students came in to complain, I would listen to their complaints and would say, "Gee, that's hard. I can see you are having a hard time fitting in the entire course with what else you have to do." Often, all their frustrations would come out as I would carefully listen and understand the best I could. I realized their frustrations were not directed at me personally—they were just frustrated over all they were attempting to do. I did not change my requirements and generally the student would return the next day with the assignment done.

> *The teacher listened to the complaints of the students, validated their feelings and left the responsibility where it belonged.*

One thing helps me keep my requirements high and that is the letters I have received from my students who have graduated. They have thanked me for what I expected out of them and stated they now see how it has helped them in their graduate work or occupation.

This wise teacher set a standard, explained it at the beginning of the course, and left the responsibility to fill the requirements with those who signed up for the course. She listened to the complaints of the students, validated their feelings and left the responsibility where it belonged. Too often when we jump in and want to help someone, we try to take their responsibility to alleviate their discomfort. We think this is helping when all it often does is further frustrate the other person. This teacher could have cut down the requirements and made it easier for the students. It would have made that short time easier but would have made the future more difficult because the student would not have been as prepared to meet the job challenges.

VALIDATION—A LIFE SAVER

Doctors face life and death challenges often during their careers. One doctor reported that he never expected to face the challenge of someone standing in his office threatening to kill him. He related the following:

> The law requires that doctors report incidents of child abuse which can result in the children being put in protective custody. The day before this incident happened, I had had to make a report of abuse to the state agency. The next day I walked into my private office and there stood the father of the abused children with a gun pointed directly at me. He said, "You took away my children. They were my life! And now I am going to take away your life."
> I have never been as frightened as I was at that moment. I knew if I said the wrong thing I was dead. So I validated him by saying, "I guess if I were you I would want

to kill me too." He stood there for a few moments then started to cry and gradually lowered the gun and sat down.

In some people, extreme stress can cause behavior that is not normal. This father could only see the fact that they had taken his children away. He could not see how his actions had caused the need for protective custody. Some people are looking for someone else to blame rather than take responsibility for their own actions. This doctor saw the need to listen and understand. He told me, "I have thought about the incident often and realized that if I hadn't understood that man and his feelings I would probably be dead."

BELIEVE IN YOUR EMPLOYEES

With each person that is hired for a particular job, there are two sets of expectations and wants. The employee wants to do a good job and expects to be well trained to be able to meet the company's expectations. The employer wants the employee to find success in doing a good job and expects the employee to work hard. As I mentioned earlier in this chapter, every employer wants each employee to feel that she is an integral part of the overall operation. The employer can enhance this feeling if he takes the time to listen to his employees, their needs, desires, and suggestions.

When an employee sees a problem in either a process or a policy of the company, an owner or manager would do well to listen. The management can encourage improvement by how they respond to the employee. I heard one employer say to an employee, "Look, you are not paid to think. You are here to just do your job." By taking this attitude, much valuable input is lost. If the employer learns to validate the interest of each employee and ask validating questions, the company has the best chance to grow and succeed. By validating, he can tap into an individual's expertise and experience. It takes personal strength and self-belief on both the employer's and the employee's part to do this. Many companies say they have the policy yet often lose it in the day-to-day contact. Sometimes the employer doesn't take time to listen or show trust in the employee.

For instance, in a manufacturing plant, one line assembler found himself and others having to wait for some parts. Rather than just waste time talking, he saw the problem, devised a plan, and went to his manager. If the manager had merely given the employee lip service and told him he would think about a solution, it is likely that nothing would have changed and the company would have continued to lose man hours. Instead, realizing he did not have to solve all the problems himself, the manager listened to the problem and *asked if the employee had a solution.* The employee showed the plan he had been working on. It made sense to the manager though it involved an expenditure of money and equipment. They implemented the plan and it resulted in a significant labor savings to the company.

Not all suggestions are possible. For example, if equipment is older or slightly outdated and an employee requests newer equipment, the business may not have the resources to replace the older equipment. It seems as soon as you buy a new piece of equipment someone comes out with a newer model. Nevertheless, such a request could be responded to in a positive and accepting manner. It isn't the fact of being turned down that invalidates an employee. It is the *way* he is turned down. For instance, a print shop owner was approached by his press operator concerning the difficulty of a particular print job. He suggested that the shop needed a more up-to-date press. The owner asked him if the job could be done on the existing press and the worker stated it would be much easier and faster on a new press. Instead of replying in a disgusted manner, the owner could validate the employee by saying,

> *When an employee brings up a problem, the most validating thing is to ask the question, "What do you think could be done?"*

"That will be a challenge. I can see we do need a newer press and the job will be more difficult with what we have. I wish replacing it were possible; however, I am not able to do that now. I will appreciate your best work."

Most people respond positively to being listened to, validated, and appreciated. When an employee brings up a problem, the most validating thing is to ask the question, "What do you think could be done?" If the employee has a suggestion, *listen*. If the employee doesn't have a solution, then maybe the validating question could be, "Would you give it some thought and bring me some ideas? You are close to the problem and may see some things I don't see. Thanks for your interest." This indirectly says to the employee, "I need your experience, I value your ideas, and I want to work with you."

Often, business owners and managers have the tendency to immediately come up with a solution to every problem or complaint. This is a constant burden and can lead to managerial burnout. Developing workers who are loyal to the business and who can look for solutions as well as problems is important. Alert and dedicated employees can help shoulder part of the burden and provide solutions to problems and challenges that might not be readily visible unless you work with it every day.

BEGIN TODAY

Turn back to chapter six and review the validating phrases and questions. Pick some that fit you and see where they can be used in your business. Remember, there is commonality of needs, desires, and feelings. It doesn't matter where in the business you work—a difficult task is a difficult task. Walk with the other person where they are, acknowledging what they are feeling. Watch how the attitude changes when you validate by listening and understanding.

Chapter Fifteen

————·••·•··——

Conclusion

DO IT!

It is my hope at this point that you have begun freeing yourself from the burden of thinking you are responsible for solving everybody's problems and that you have already begun using the principles of validation. I recognize that effectively using these principles takes practice. It is not easy to let go and let those you care about solve their own problems when you are sure you have the right answer for them. Resisting this urge and leaving the responsibility with the person it belongs to will be the best help you can give. Allow yourself time to grow as you use and perfect these skills.

What I don't want to occur is for you to read this book, get all excited about its concepts and then not implement them. Please don't let that happen. I want you to experience the joy these concepts can bring to you and those you care about. I want you to experience a new depth of love and caring in all your relationships. If it takes referring back to different chapters as you consciously work at implementing validation into your everyday conversation, then I hope you will do it. It will be worth every effort.

REVIEW

As a simple review and to help cement these concepts in your mind I have listed eight key questions below. The answer follows each question and, to test your memory, I suggest you cover the answer until you have answered the question.

1. What is validation?

   The ability to walk emotionally with another person without trying to change his or her thinking or direction.

2. What are the Four Rules of Validation?

   • LISTEN (by giving your full attention)
   • LISTEN (to the feelings being expressed)
   • LISTEN (to the needs being expressed)
   • UNDERSTAND (by putting yourself in
        the other person's shoes as best you can)

3. What is the universal need of every human being?

To know that I am of worth, my feelings matter, and someone really cares about me.

4. What is the underlying principle that allows a person to effectively validate someone else?

A recognition that I do not have the power to make anything all better for anyone else. I can offer my help, but I cannot make it all better.

5. Where does the responsibility for someone's problem lie?

With the person who has the problem.

6. What are the four key elements of effective boundary setting?

Be kind, gentle, respectful, and firm.

7. When is the right time to teach?

Out of the heat of the moment. Not when a person is pouring out their feelings to you and not when either of you are upset.

8. Give two good validating phrases and
     questions.

(This answer is almost endless. Here are four
     of my favorites:)
- That's got to be hard.
- I think I might have felt the same way.
- How did you feel about that?
- What do you think might work?

A SONG TO LEAN ON

When my wife and I share these principles
of validation at our seminars I usually conclude by
singing a song my wife and Janice Kapp Perry
wrote, titled *Let Me Be That Someone*. Since I
can't sing it to you now, I'll share the words here.

Let Me Be That Someone

When you know someone loves you,
     That a friend is always there,
     The sun shines much brighter
     And there's music in the air.

When you know someone's listening
     With an understanding heart
     Then life seems much better,
     The road is not so hard.

So let me be that someone who will stay.
And let me be the bright spot in your day.
I'd like to be your friend,
I'll try to understand,
And we'll find happiness along the way.

When your world seems too heavy,
When your stars no longer shine,
Come sit here beside me
And we'll spend a little time.

I can't make things all better,
For that's really up to you,
But sometimes the sharing
Can help you make it through.

So let me be that someone who will stay.
And let me be the bright spot in your day.
I'd like to be your friend,
I'll try to understand,
And we'll find happiness along the way.

— *Joy Saunders Lundberg*

Joy and I have written this book jointly with the hope that it would make a difference in your life. Life is too short to be weighed down with problems that are not our responsibility and that we are unable to solve. Through sharing and validation we believe as the song above states, "I'll try to understand, and we'll find happiness along the way."

Gary & Joy Lundberg

WORKS CITED

1. "Valid, validate, validation." Webster's third New International Dictionary of the English Language Unabridged. 1986 ed. Merriam - Webster. Philippines. 2529-2530

2. Casey, Kathryn. "When Children Rape." *Ladies Home Journal*, (June 1995): 116

3. Covey, Stephen R. *The 7 Habits of Highly Effective People.* New York. Simon & Schuster. 1990. 37

4. Zakich, Rhea. "Simple Secrets of Family Communication." *Readers Digest.* (August 1986): 158-159.

5. "But." *The New Dictionary of Thoughts.* Standard Book Company. 1961.

6. Covey, Stephen R. Ibid. 40

7. Guarendi, Ray. "Why Some Kids Listen." *Readers Digest,* (Jan. 1991). 120.

8. Grassli, Michaelene. "Helping Children Know Truth from Error." *Ensign,* (Nov. 1994). 12.

9. Mussen, Paul H., et al. "The First Two Years." *Child Development and Personality,* 6th ed. New York: Harper & Row, 1984. 111.

10. Yamamoto, Kaoru., et al. "Voices in Unison: Stressful Events in the Lives of Children in Six Countries." *Journal of Child Psychology and Psychiatry and Allied*

Disciplines 28 (1988): 855-64.

11. Smith, Donald. *Reader's Digest.* (April 1969).

12. Pinborough, Jan U. *Ensign.* (March, 1994). p. 49

13. Guarendi, Ray. Ibid. 119

14. *The New Testament,* Romans 12:15

15 Tannenbaum, Joe. *Male & Female Realities. Texas.* Candle Publishing Company. 1989. 117.

16 Gray, John. *Men Are from Mars, Women Are from Venus.* New York. Harper Collins. 1992. 67-68.

17. Weidner, Leo A. *Achieving the Balance.* Law Enterprises. 1988. 63.

18. Jones, E. Stanley, "Somebody Needs You." (reprint), *Guidepost Magazine.* (December 1962).

Please Share With Us

As you use the validating experiences in our book, exciting things will happen. We would love to hear about it. We continually share these new experiences in our seminars and other events. Your validating story could be the very one to inspire others to apply the principles in their lives and bring them the peace they've been searching for. Please take the few minutes needed and send your story to us. Many readers have asked how they can thank us for what our book has done for them. The best thanks we ever receive is finding out how these principles worked for our readers. If you feel comfortable doing so, please send us your experiences and your permission to use them in spoken or printed form. Mention if we can use your name or if you would rather remain anonymous. Thanks you so much.

Gary & Joy Lundberg
Riverpark Publishing Co.
4603 Imperial Beach Ave. • No. Las Vegas, NV 89030
Or: Email to garyjoy@itsnet.com

Keynote Addresses, Seminars, and Workshops

Dr. Blaine Lee, vice president and founding owner of Covey Leadership Center said, "I attended the Lundbergs' seminar and was deeply impressed with their ability to captivate their audience while presenting concepts that can significantly improve all relationships. I highly recommend their presentations."

At these seminars you will discover new ideas for:

- Improving relationships with employees, customers, and clients
- Creating genuine happiness between husband and wife
- Improving relationships with your children—including adult children—while empowering them to make responsible choices
- Effectively working with youth
- Letting go of burdens you don't need to carry

Presentations are tailored to your specific needs.
**For more information and/or to schedule Gary and Joy Lundberg
to speak at your event please use the above address or call 1-800-224-1606**

Now you can listen & learn wherever you are!

I DON'T HAVE TO MAKE EVERYTHING ALL BETTER
AUDIOTAPES

Comments from readers asking for our book on tape:

- "I love this book. Please put it on tape so I can review it daily on the way to work."
- "My husband isn't a reader, but I know he'll listen to the book on tape. He's got to have it. Hurry!"
- "When you put it on tape send me three copies immediately."

We heard you and here it is.

I Don't Have to Make Everything All Better, read by the authors, Gary and Joy Lundberg. Includes *Let Me Be That Someone,* the song written by Joy and composer Janice Kapp Perry, sung by Gary as he does at their seminars.

Abridged Version Audiotape Set
Approx. 6 hours listening time
Four 90-minute cassettes $24.95

*It's available at your favorite bookstore or
you may order using the information at the bottom of this page.*

✧   ✧   ✧   ✧   ✧

Share this relationship-saving information with a friend

For additional copies of the book **I Don't Have to Make Everything All Better,** see your favorite bookstore or you may order using the information at the bottom of this page.

Softbound cover $12.95

✧   ✧   ✧   ✧   ✧

Available at bookstores or call
1-800-311-9171
(Price does not include shipping/handling)

Counted Cross Stitch Pattern Books
Easy for the beginner and enticing for the expert.

Book 1: WORDS OF JOY
Book of 19 delightful quick-and-easy patterns to stitch and frame for your home or to give as gifts.
$5.50 each book.

Book 2: WORDS OF JOY FOR THE FAMILY
Book of 18 easy-to-do patterns, words of inspiration and appreciation, ideal to stitch for your own home or to give your loved ones.
$6.00 each book.

To order call 1-800-311-9171
(Price does not include shipping/handling)

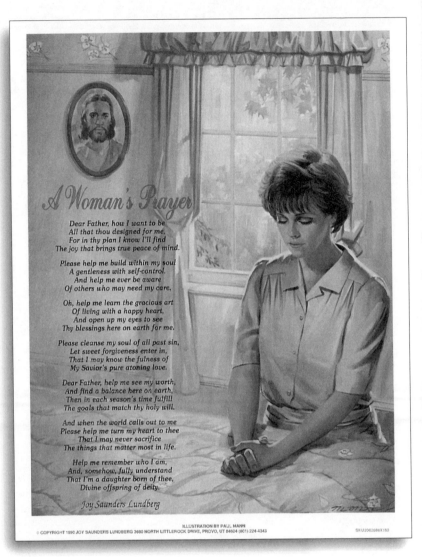

A Woman's Prayer • (8"x10" card weight) $2.00

FULL COLOR

To My Son

I look at you, my son,
And try to understand.
Where is the child?
Instead I see a man.
Then a wave of memory
Moves gently on my mind
As I walk awhile with you
Through the sands of time.

And I see you again,
A baby in my arms,
With little fists
Clenched tight,
Smiling, sometimes crying,
As I hold you
In the night.
Such an innocent
Little one,
And oh, how you
needed me then,
My son.

Then I remember how,
As a little boy,
You'd pray and play
And laugh,
And fill our home with
Immeasurable joy.
Then off to school
You went
And tried so hard
To become
All that life
Expected of you.
Even then you needed me,
My son.

Now as you walk
Through that open door,
I know you don't need me
So much anymore.
And that's okay,
For I can see
You've become the man
I hoped you would be.
Keep your faith strong,
For your work's just begun,
And never stop needing
The Lord, my son.

Joy Saunders Lundberg

To My Son • (8"x10" card weight) $2.00

SINGLE PASTEL COLOR

To order call 1-800-311-9171
(Price does not include shipping/handling)

To My Daughter

I see you standing
At the threshold of
Tomorrow
And my mind is filled with
Tender thoughts,
Laced with a touch
Of sorrow,

For you're no longer
My little girl,
The child who climbed
Upon my knee
To kiss my cheek
And bring the gift
Of happiness
To me.

Through the years
I've wiped your tears
And chased away
Your childhood fears.
I've felt a pride
I can't describe
As I have watched you grow.
But now the time has come
When I must let you go.

And other lives will
Now be blessed
By your sweet love
And gentleness.
Keep your faith
And trust in God,
Hold fast to all
That's good and true.
And never forget,
His love and mine
Will always
Be with you.

Joy Saunders Lundberg

To My Daughter • (8"x10" card weight) $2.00

SINGLE PASTEL COLOR

To order call 1-800-311-9171
(Price does not include shipping/handling)

A Time To Mourn

I know I can't erase
The pain you feel today
Oh, how I wish my love for you
Could make it go away.

They say that time will heal,
And I'm sure it will, somehow,
But until then no one can know
The hurt you feel right now.

Please let me be the one
To take you by the hand,
To wipe away your saddest tears
And try to understand.

I'll listen as you share
Sweet memories from your heart,
I'll walk with you as you begin
To make a fresh new start.

And though your precious one
Has gone to Heaven's home,
With God's eternal love, and mine,
You'll never be alone.

Joy Saunders Lundberg

A Time to Mourn • (8"x10" card weight) $2.00

FULL COLOR

THE UNIVERSAL NEED

There is a need within every person to feel that

I AM OF WORTH

MY FEELINGS MATTER

and

SOMEONE REALLY CARES ABOUT ME

From *I Dont Have To Make Everything All Better* © Riverpark Publishing Co.

PERSONAL BOUNDARIES ARE YOUR VALUE SYSTEM IN ACTION.

In setting effective boundaries, you must be:

- KIND
- GENTLE
- RESPECTFUL
- FIRM

The first three make the last one work.

From *I Don't Have To Make Everything All Better* © Riverpark Publishing Co.

I DON'T HAVE TO MAKE EVERYTHING ALL BETTER

From *I Don't Have To Make Everything All Better* © Riverpark Publishing Co.

THE FOUR RULES OF VALIDATION

1. LISTEN by giving your full attention.

2. LISTEN to the emotions being expressed.

3. LISTEN to the needs being expressed.

4. UNDERSTAND by putting yourself in the other person's shoes as best you can.

The greatest gift you can give your children

is

Parents Who Love Each Other.